Strategy, Leadership and the Soul

RESILIENCE, RESPONSIVENESS AND REFLECTION FOR A GLOBAL ECONOMY

Jennifer Sertl and Koby Huberman

Published in this edition in 2010 by:

Triarchy Press
Station Offices
Axminster
Devon
EX13 5PF
United Kingdom

+44 (0)1297 631456
info@triarchypress.com
www.triarchypress.com

A catalogue record for this book is available from the British Library.

ISBN: 978-0-9562631-9-3

I was asked if I had met Merlin the Magician and I said
Absolutely! And his name is now Napier Collyns.

Contents

Contents

Acknowledgements

I am the collective of the company I keep. How lucky am I to be surrounded by such wonderful people: Tom Hill, Max Carey, Bruce Peters, Mitch Thrower, Paul Weinstein. My life has been enriched by knowing you.

Everyone deserves a coach or a confidant. I so appreciate the safe enquiry I experience with Ann, who helps me question my own motives and actions to seek wiser choices.

In my community I have enjoyed working with several brave, strong, and clear leaders—especially James Tabbi, Jim Goff, Rick Plympton and Mike Mandina. Your leadership is why I continue to do what I do. Koby Huberman, Alison Melvin and Harvey Ardman—you helped my voice have wings to travel the global distance. Thank you.

Finally, my family. Eric, you are my rock. Thank you for your strength. Sienna, you give me beauty every day with your smile. Hannah, you give me faith every day with your gentle spirit. Griffin, you give me presence every day—when you make me chase you to get you dressed.

Jennifer Sertl

My many friends—diverse people, from many cultures and with different languages and religions—are the source of energy I value most. I have been lucky to work with amazing people: leaders and entrepreneurs who put their minds and hearts at work for business prosperity, economic prosperity, peace-making and bridge building. My colleagues and friends Shmil Levi, Benny Levin, Shlomo Dovrat and Shlomo Shamir— you have been a continuous inspiration for me in the past 20 years when thinking and conceptualizing this book. For the long hours of stimulating and enriching conversation, I would like to thank Ofer Levy, Tal Ronen, Rivki Stern, Tova Averbuch, Shay Ben-Yosef and Avner Haramati. Brave visionary partners—Yuval Rabin and Yoav Levi—have taught me a lesson in patience and commitment to a vision. And brave social transformation leaders, all working for the sake of building bridges between Jews and Arabs in Israel—Dov Lautman, Fadoul Mazzawi, Mohammad Darawshe, Avital Geva, Ibtisam Mahameed, Saeed Abu-Shaqra, Anat Livne and many others—you have all enlightened me to new horizons of human empathy. I thank all of you for rare and great moments, thoughts and ideas, and for allowing me to witness and be part of your journey.

Many thanks to Mike Filderbaum, Yoram Yahav and Schlomo Meital for encouraging me to write this book. And special thanks to a very special person—my friend and partner Naftali Shimrat—for his wisdom, energy and friendship.

Special thanks to Jennifer—without you, this book would not have been created. Thanks for teaching me a lesson by re-spelling "passion" for me.

And the greatest admiration to my family. Tal, I owe it all to you, the star in our life—a person who has demonstrated more leadership, more strategy and especially more soul than any other person I know. And to the wonderful kids—Shachar, Gil, Ron and Orr—you all bring light, happiness and music to this world—and constantly remind me of what's really important in life.

Koby Huberman

Foreword—by Napier Collyns

I first met Jennifer Sertl and Koby Huberman by chance at Forum 21 in 2005 at a beautiful resort on the French Riviera. With many others we were wondering what the new century would be like and what each of us would have to do to adapt to it. It was a wonderful intellectual feast. Koby was speaking about Open Space Technology as a means of Arabs and Israelis getting together on the only thing they have in common— not wanting their children to die in battle. And Jennifer and I were on a panel: If you Want to Change the World: Change Your Life! (Thank you, Paul Weinstein!) After we had gone home to Israel, Rochester and San Francisco, respectively, we began to correspond, and to listen to and learn from each other.

Our conversations, reinforced by the events we have witnessed in the last few years, brought to mind my arrival in America as a graduate history student at Brown. It was 1951, and Edmund S. Morgan and Donald Fleming were conducting a year-long seminar on the Gilded Age and the robber barons. We never thought such an age would ever be repeated, with all the wicked behavior of leading industrialists and bankers. But as we have seen, such lessons are not always learned or digested.

It is clearly time to rethink capitalism—both the good aspects and the bad. Despite all the efforts of business schools and the writings of eminent economists and historians, the 'Enronization' of America continues, and we need to find new Roosevelts, both Theodore and Franklin, to put a stop to it.

Now Jennifer and Koby have written a book that provides abundant guidance on how to create an atmosphere in which new, humane organizations can grow and flourish—organizations of all types and sizes with appropriate values, incentives and strategies that sustain and work for individuals, families, businesses, philanthropies, and governments. Many of the bad habits of modern capitalism can be overcome by paying attention to and applying the authors' inspiring and rewarding ideas.

Back in 1987, I was one of a few friends who started Global Business Network, before the Internet and social media had begun to profoundly influence the way people think and share values. In those days, we brought together remarkable, visionary people from a variety of disciplines to meet with executives in major corporations in order to exchange and explore views about the future, using both early forms of electronic conversation and face-to-face interactions. This new book captures many of the lessons we learned on a daily basis about stimulating and adapting to change and gives them a universal applicability. It is a book to carry with you, to read on airplanes or the subway, a chapter or a paragraph at a time. But it is also a call to action. Its insights are applicable to so many aspects of life: to self development, family relationships, small and large businesses, and indeed to the future of all organizations in every sector and in every part of the world. Read the book—and change your life!

Napier Collyns worked in the international energy business for many years before joining Peter Schwartz, Stewart Brand, Jay Ogilvy and Lawrence Wilkinson in starting Global Business Network, now part of the Monitor Group, in 1987.

Preface

If you stroll down the aisles of the nearest big-box bookstore, you'll find shelf after shelf crammed full of management and leadership books. Some are timeless classics, some written by famous authors, some are recent best-sellers, and some have inspired changes in major organizations and given birth to seminars, even college courses.

All of them, even the best of them, are missing the single most important ingredient in management and leadership: you.

By "you" we don't mean the generalized, non-specific grammatically convenient "you". We mean *you* personally, the unique man or woman who must make day-to-day and moment-to-moment decisions, the very particular individual who wants to become a better leader and who wants to steer his or her organization toward greater things.

As a rule, "best practice" management books and theories prescribe certain behaviors and attitudes for their readers. This book is no exception. But there is a crucial difference.

What we prescribe is based on who you really are, on the *authentic* you. Our most urgent request is that you plumb the depths of your intrinsic self and act in accordance with it. And with equal urgency, we ask that you acknowledge and respect the humanity of everyone you deal with.

We ask this because our decades of experience as executives in global corporations, as consultants with small-to-medium-sized businesses and other organizations, tells us that the times are demanding no less.

To put it another way, we are convinced that if you do not act in accord with your innermost self, and you do not respect the humanity of others, your chances of personal success, and your chances of leading your organization to success, will be significantly reduced.

This was not always the case. In the past, the social, technological and economic environment was conducive to standardized, or even regimented, behavior. Unfortunately, many organizations—and consultants—are not aware of how profoundly the world has changed. They believe there is a "plug and play" leadership model that will work for you (or anyone else), if only you obey the right top brand consultant or internalize the right Harvard Business Review article. That's mainstream thinking even now.

This book does not belong to that tradition. We don't believe that one size fits all. We know that everyone is different, and that the differences must be recognized, accounted for and built upon, and that it is these differences that contain what is unique and most creative about you and about those you work for and work with. This is the approach that maximizes your resources.

We want to give you reason to trust your judgment. And toward that end, we plan to show you how to sharpen your senses, and to ask yourself provocative questions that will help you better understand how you think, how you sense and how you navigate reality. We plan to show you how to best use your individuality and your humanity to heighten your chances of success and fulfillment.

Three Big Ideas

As the title indicates, our book explores and illuminates three main ideas:

1. **Strategy.** We are convinced that, in order to lead your company in the business environment of the 21st century, it is essential for you to master the ability to invent your company's future, particularly in the current rapidly changing strategic landscapes of your business. Therefore, the old ways of designing a strategy need to change—you will need to *constantly* rethink your strategy, not just once every few years.

2. **Leadership.** Leadership styles and challenges have dramatically changed and will continue to change from the Old World models. In order to handle successfully the age's enormous complexity and to improve your ability in the role of a leader, you will need to become highly skilled at sensing relevance in all areas of life and business, and to create synergistic relationships between all parties.

3. **Soul.** To accomplish these two things, we contend that your values and inner beliefs should be in harmony with that of your organization and vice versa. Only in this way, we believe, can you maximize your organization's power and efficiency and create a working environment that allows you and your people to find satisfaction and fulfillment in your work and your lives. And we further assert that organizations—every one of them—have their own soul—the internal, intangible yet extremely present and powerful set of inner beliefs that make the organization one of a kind. We believe that recognition of this has immense value, and alignment of this "soul" factor across customers, employees and business partners is a fundamental necessity for success.

What You Can Expect

We're not going to ask you to take our convictions on faith. We are going to share with you the observations and insights we have gathered over the years in the process of talking to hundreds of organizations around the world.

In doing this, we look beyond the superficial observation that everything is changing, faster than ever, to explain *why* the business environment is changing, what's causing it to change and what these changes imply.

First, we look at how the organization has evolved over the last 150 years or so, and at which factors have controlled and guided that almost Darwinian evolution. And we will focus on the 21st century and on the organizational model it has given birth to, a phenomenon we call the *transorganization*.

Secondly, we describe what it is that makes transorganizations different from their predecessors, and especially how the old paradigm of "command and control" is giving way to a new model, where the guiding principle is "communicate and enroll".

We demonstrate what is likely to happen to organizations and leaders that continue as before—operating as if the world is essentially the same as it was twenty or thirty years ago when they received their MBAs and went through their formative corporate experiences, and acting like generals who still believe that only the cavalry are an important battlefield asset. And we will show you why many people born before 1980, or thereabouts, are burdened with this inclination.

We then consider, at length, the new kind of leader—the CEO or COO or perhaps the Board Chairman of the transorganization, someone we call a *transleader*. We examine the successful transleader's human and personal characteristics as well as the practices that make transleadership work.

In that process, we hope to help you navigate your transformation from conventional leadership to transleadership, in order to put you and your organization in the right position to ride the organization tsunami of the 21st century toward unprecedented growth and success.

In guiding you through your personal transformation, we will look at the concept of agility, deconstructing it into its constituent elements— resilience, responsiveness and reflection—and show you how to strengthen these fundamental behavioral skills. We explore the ins and outs of strategic thinking and decision-making and what you need to do to be sure you have a reasonably good idea of reality, as it affects your organization and your leadership.

We will talk about the role that your organizational energy (i.e. your organization's "wattage", capacity and potential to perform, and not just its performance) plays in your organization's success or failure. We will explore the parameters of organizational health.

It is our aim is to help you transform your life—internally as a human being and externally as a leader—so that you lead a more fulfilled and more prosperous life and your organization has the maximum chance for success.

We will also consider the major societal, technological and business trends that are likely to propel the continued evolution of the organization, and examine what the organization of the near future will look like.

Who Should Read This Book

The social, economic, technological and political transformations of the last twenty years have triggered the collapse of the old order of the organization—the old hierarchy, the old structure, the old notion that knowledge and experience trumps everything when it comes to leadership.

The old methods aren't working as well as they once did, and this has triggered a crisis of leadership for today's organizations—schools, communities, countries, non-governmental entities and, of course, business organizations of all types and sizes. This book is aimed at updating and reviving leadership skills for the entire panorama of organizations, and for everyone who is or would be a leader in today's world. It is our intent to stimulate people and organizations by giving them relevant questions to ask themselves and relevant actions to take, and by providing them with the intellectual case for transformation.

So, we believe that this book will make valuable reading for the young American entrepreneur who has just completed her MBA, for an experienced Chinese businessman who wants to expand into Europe, for a young Arab executive in Jordan who wants to develop a global network of distributors for his company's new software application, or for a veteran Brazilian CEO who wants to open an office in Russia.

This is the book which will show a young Italian leading a health-care assistance NGO, an Egyptian civil society leader, a Russian mayor and an Indian university president that the challenges they face can be very much like those found in the business world, and may sometimes be more complex. It will show them that strategy, leadership and soul are very much the same, no matter what the setting.

If you see the world as your business theater, if you are eager to meet people, eager to drive success, eager to lead a winning network of teams, passionate about leading a 21st century organization, this book is for you.

If you want to expand your horizons beyond your store of knowledge and experience, if you want to reach new people, new cultures, and new levels of global participation, this book is for you.

If you want to understand how to meet the challenges of our time, if you want to get ahead of the ever-accelerating speed of change, if you want to get a handle on the complexity of the 21st century, this book is for you.

If you aren't impressed with the *7 Surefire Steps To Success* or *How I Led My Company to Victory* best-sellers, if you want more depth and no longer have much respect for the tricks and manipulations of 20th century management, or if you are tired of being told what to do and would rather think about what you're doing and, in this way, to discover what works for you, this book is for you.

This book is specifically aimed at the CEOs or executive leaders of small-to-medium-sized businesses (SMBs), although it is equally valid, we think, for the leaders of the divisions or departments of large corporations that, by themselves, function like SMBs, let's say, the manager of GE's engine division, or Caterpillar Nigeria or the natural beverages division of Nestlé in Europe.

There is a mindset that comes with the historical, environmental, economic and political issues as a set of collective experiences. This book is particularly aimed at Generation Xers and Boomers who at this time are between the ages of 30 and 65. Our intent is to share perspectives that help those who became adults in the traditional business model to adapt more quickly to current market trends and be more able to anticipate the future.

And this book is decidedly *not* aimed at people of any age who are unwilling or unable to change, people who have found their safe harbors and can't be convinced to leave them, those for whom the words "new" and "change" are synonymous with "threat" and "danger".

Most importantly, if you are willing to admit that to be a successful leader in the 21st century you must have a sense of humor, a sense of humility and a passion for learning, then this book is for you. This book is a call to consciousness. And being a successful leader means much more than just making profits—going forward, it will require the deep understanding of the social fabric, the diversity of communities, the world of philanthropy, and the commitment to a shared society, shared planet and shared humanity.

How Should You Read This Book?

All authors, in the back of their minds, have an image of people reading their book—faces lighting up as they share an insight, chuckling at a *bon mot*, eyebrows knit—then smooth—as they puzzle out a complicated thought.

Our vision is somewhat different. If you react the way we hope you will, you'll read slowly, pausing frequently, asking yourself how it applies to you specifically, or to your organization.

If we've done our job, every page in this book will lead you to think about yourself, about the way you operate, about your relationships, about your organization and about your vision, both for yourself and for your company. We hope that you will never look at the world... or your organization... or your employees... or your customers... or yourself... in quite the same way again.

How are we going to accomplish this? By presenting a world view that is absolutely obvious to some—mostly younger people—but completely invisible to others, because they've been brought up in a different era.

Before you read this book, ask yourself what you hope to gain from it and how you expect to apply it. We want you to read with intention—and we think you shouldn't waste your time if you know you're not going to *use* what you read.

We hope to provoke you. We hope to raise uncomfortable questions. We don't even mind if you get angry or strongly disagree with something we say—so long as you consider it seriously. We hope to alter—to broaden—your thinking.

Part One: The Evolution of the Organization

In the middle of the road of my life, I awoke in a dark wood,
Where the true way was wholly lost.
Dante

To the casual observer, it might seem that small-to-medium-sized companies haven't changed all that much since the Industrial Revolution —bigger, yes, more mechanized, automated and computerized, certainly, more spread out geographically, of course, but nonetheless, basically the same.

This is a misconception. Corporations and other organizations have changed dramatically over the years, in parallel with human culture and society. They've changed and grown, or they've disappeared because they are no longer relevant. And they haven't stopped changing and probably never will, just as society never stops changing.

If the past is any indication, nothing is more essential to an organization— almost any kind of organization, public or private, profit-making or non-profit—than to detect the advent and the character of the next round of changes, if it is to have any chance to thrive, or even survive.

What will organizations look like five or ten years from now? How will their structure and organization differ from those of today's organizations? What differences will there be in their behavior, both internally and externally? How can CEOs make sure their organizations respond and adjust to change, or better yet stay ahead of it?

This evolution of the organization has been almost Darwinian. Each new iteration has succeeded the previous for a very good reason: it has generated more wealth, on an annual basis. Outmoded organizations have either changed, or been absorbed by the new kinds of companies, or have simply disappeared.

Organizational changes have been accelerating, and the alterations have become more and more profound. And each new organizational generation has dominated the marketplace for a shorter period than its predecessor. How long the next one will last is anyone's guess, but the odds are it will be superseded even more quickly than it sped past its predecessor.

Prior to the Industrial Revolution, which began in the mid 1800s in Great Britain, companies were organized in simple and, from today's viewpoint, primitive ways. The entire hierarchy consisted, at most, of owners, managers, foremen and laborers. Then came the Industrial Revolution and the birth of what we call the "F-Organization".

The F-Organization (1850-1940): Founders, Families and Fortunes

The Industrial Age gave birth to the first corporate organizations, companies built around factories involved in turning raw materials into products and distributing these products over increasingly wider areas.

These progenitors of the modern corporation were almost always the creation of single individuals or partnerships: men who had developed new products or found ways to employ the early industrial technology to mass produce products that were formerly the sole province of artisans.

We call these F-Organizations because they were managed and driven by their founder or the family members that succeeded him. They created textiles, china, farm implements, pig iron, processed foods, armaments and other manufactured goods.

F-Organizations were highly entrepreneurial, with single core competencies and a patriarchal management style. The work force was not considered a partner in the enterprise; it was merely a resource. Employees could expect lifetime employment, but without significant bargaining power this meant long hours, subsistence wages, strict adherence to company dictates and practically no chance for advancement.

As technology evolved and the marketplace expanded, F-Organizations grew larger and larger and more and more complex and their power and wealth expanded in kind.

By the end of the last great economic contraction in about 1940 and during World War II, a new generation of organizations emerged, which we would recognize as modern organizations. Since then, according to our analysis, organizational evolutions have come faster and faster. We believe that the world has seen no less than four organizational generations in the last 70 years, and that a fifth is on the way.

The S-Organization (1940-1970): Structure and Security

The immediate successor to the F-Organization was the S-Organization. The modern organization was born at a critical moment, at the end of a depression and the beginning of the most horrendous war in history. Not surprisingly, business leaders sought to enlist and reassure employees by building companies that were based on providing a stable structure, in which every employee had a clear space, an assigned job and workplace. This organizational change dovetailed nicely with the way society was structuring itself, creating a clear separation of responsibility and identity between its various sectors: government, manufacturing, services, utilities, transportation and households.

Internally, S-Organizations were built around seniority. Those with experience and long years of service generally received the promotions to higher positions. This was in the best interest of the organization because their experiences remained useful for decades—for their entire working careers. Thanks to these experienced and knowledgeable people, these organizations owned practically all the skills they needed to run the business, and in their operations, they emphasized self-reliance and self-sufficiency.

This era was marked by a scientific approach towards individual and team behavior. Management style was a key issue and the subject of many books and seminars. Efficiency was the watchword, and it trumped almost every other aspect of management.

S-Organizations, those that survived, evolved into a new generation of organizations, the P-Organization, leaving remnants and traces of their former selves. The elements of "structuralism" that can be found in today's organizations are the genetic leftovers from S-Organizations, in much the same way human beings carry genetic fragments of previous evolutionary stages. And, in the organization, these fragmented leftovers often have considerable power—usually of the counter-productive variety.

The P-Organization (1970-1995): Products, Performance and Profits

The P-age is the organizational environment in which many of today's business leaders went to business school. There they were introduced to the 4P or 7P marketing model. This was designed to guide organizations in a more intensely competitive period. Marketing became the essence of business—marketing with the power of promotional tools, creative pricing and the art of positioning products.

Organizations were now focusing on the practical side of management. Structure was still important, but the new keywords were performance, profitability and productivity, and the implementation of policies, processes, procedures and priorities. Organizations operated according to the unity paradigm, everyone in the company looking and acting the same.

Combined with increased urbanization and large-scale manufacturing, the P-age provided a new potential for business growth. Instead of just building infrastructure and meeting customers' basic needs, new products created new needs. Technological progress became the driving force in the competitive marketplace. It enabled corporations not only to provide solutions and meet customer needs, and to push products to new levels of performance and productivity, but also to find new ways to attract and please the consumer. The result: demands that simply did not exist before.

In order to manage these changes, to properly interact with their customers, to protect their turf and the market position they had captured, corporations had to develop new public relations and advertising practices. But the product was the key. The intangibles were few and of lesser importance to management.

It was an age of power building, power use and powerful leadership. The personality of the leader became more and more important to the organization's ultimate success, and CEOs dominated their corporate culture, becoming business celebrities and stars, both within the corporation and externally. Among the examples of this phenomenon, Jack Welch, the former head of General Electric, and Bill Gates of Microsoft. Typically, the CEOs of P-Organizations were experienced, knowledgeable and sometimes heroic.

The P-age was characterized by other p-words as well, not all of which were positive: for instance, perfectionism, pressure, paranoia, patronizing and paternalistic. The combination made companies inflexible, afraid of failure, and unable to change quickly. They operated reactively, making changes when they felt they had no choice. These major changes often took 18-24 months to implement and were often already outdated by the time they were put into place.

The E-Organization (1995-2002):
An Exceptional Electronic Evolutionary Episode

On one afternoon in September 1999, the market cap of eToys.inc surpassed that of Toys-R-Us—although eToys was losing money on a revenue volume which was a fraction of Toys-R-Us, while Toys-R-Us was a profitable business.

How did that happen?

We believe that the business world was attacked by an e-virus, which led to the emergence of a new kind of enterprise. The enterprise was a business that looked at earnings in a different way—not the GAAP way, not the cash way, but through the eyeballs.

During the seven short years between 1995 and 2002, you could take almost any business model, decorate it with "e-something" lingo and put it out on the marketplace— and the venture capitalists (VCs) would begin to circle, money in their hands.

Business models? No one cared. Conventional profit and loss calculations? No longer applicable. The world was no longer in the P-age of the last 25 years, it had e-volved into the e-world, in which everything—especially products and profits—would be delivered with the help of that most miraculous highway, the Internet. Or so everyone thought.

And the E-Organization leader was very different from previous corporate leaders. He (or she) was young, anti-authoritarian, informal, a risk-taker, inexperienced, experimental and, sometimes unfortunately, wildly over-optimistic.

As a result, the organization itself was haphazard and ad hoc, a collection of freelancers with various levels of commitment to the organizational goal, and sharing many of the leader's characteristics.

The e-world was real enough, but the conclusions everybody had drawn about it were an illusion, and the illusion didn't last long. eToys, for instance, turned into a pumpkin in the year 2000, after the 1999-2000 holiday season. It was easy enough to order toys via the Internet, but not so easy to provide enough customer service to deal with erroneous shipments, broken boxes, and other product problems, or enough operational knowledge to deal with surging demands. Before long, VCs realized that before they invested in e-companies, they had to weigh business plans and make rational measurements of the possibilities.

And so the e-bubble burst, leaving many casualties, among them the VCs that allowed themselves to be drawn into the fantasy that conventional ways of doing business had gone the way of the dodo. The E-Organization was a necessary, if not inevitable, step in the evolution of the organization, and it lasted only until its flaws and limitations became obvious.

Nonetheless, the E-Organization had many useful elements. It showed the world that some important and profitable operations can be and should be delivered as technology-driven interactions (web, contact center, etc.), and consequently, in the past decade, organizations have developed great infrastructure systems to enable such interactions.

Some of the stronger E-Organizations were able to survive the bursting bubble, in part because their business models fit the parameters better, and in part because they were able to combine elements of e-thinking with the paradigm of profitable performance.

Companies such as eBay and Amazon showed that e-businesses could become prodigiously profitable and, in a few instances, even better at value-building than some of largest and most powerful P-Organizations. In terms of percentage increase in stock value, Google and e-Bay consistently outperformed GE and IBM from early 1999 to late 2009.

The vast majority of E-Organizations simply evaporated when the bubble burst, taking with them the investors' money, as well as their founders' over-optimistic dreams. E-Organizations turned out to be an anomaly in the evolution of organizations, and a brief one at that.

However, the failure of E-Organizations did not reverse the evolution of the organization. P-Organizations persisted, and the most forward-thinking among them adopted some of the characteristics of the E-Organization. The era that had given birth to the P-Organization, however, was quickly passing. The world was undergoing profound social, economic and technological changes, and at a rate unprecedented in human history.

Corporate Organizational Structure Eras

Era	Time Period	Key Characteristics
F-Organization	1850-1940	Farmers, Families, Fortunes • single core competence • patriarchy as management style • lifetime employment
S-Organization	1940-1970	Structure & Security • stability was the key target • leadership became hierarchical • seniority was valued • focus was efficiency
P-Organization	1970-1995	Products, Performance, Profits • policies and procedures • rise of the MBA • systems became more important than people
E-Organization	1995-2002	Electronic Evolution • e-business and dot.com • e-commerce • everybody can play

Part Two: The 21ˢᵗ Century— The World Transformed

The universe is transformation; our life is what our thoughts make it.
Marcus Aurelius

In 1963, Bob Dylan wrote, "The times, they are a-changing". But it's unlikely that even he realized that, from that moment on, the times would never stop changing and that the changes would be far more profound than anyone anticipated, or that they would affect practically every aspect of life—from our personal relationships to the relationships between nations, from our inner lives to our lives in the material world.

A kind of perfect storm has swept over the entire world: a coincidence of factors large and small, predictable and totally unexpected, and it's much larger than the one Bob Dylan wrote about more than 40 years ago. Most importantly for our purposes, it has altered the basic foundations of the marketplace, the corporation, the community and the organization. Those who recognize and embrace these changes have the best chance to succeed. Those who don't are in serious danger.

The Technological Tsunami

Time was when the fabric of everyday life remained pretty much the same, generation after generation. Then, in the last half of the 19ᵗʰ century, with the advent of the factory, train transportation, the telegraph, the telephone and electricity, the changes began to quicken. However, life remained pretty much the same for the better part of a generation. Grandfathers and grandsons inhabited the same world.

For people in the business world, it was much the same. They joined or founded a company, and it grew and they grew with it according to the original set of rules. Business practices, production technology, distribution, marketing techniques all evolved, but what the young executive began learning, let's say in the 1920s, was still pretty much applicable in the business world of the 1940s when he became the CEO.

Getting one business school degree, learning one trade, mastering the ropes at one or two organizations—that was enough for a lifetime, at the end of which you got your gold watch and took the wife to see the Eiffel Tower.

Then, sometime in the mid 1960s, career life expectancy began to shrink. New waves of technology began washing over the world of business— jet travel, the transistor, automation, mainframe record-keeping, and vastly improved communication. It was no longer enough for executives to master business as they had known it; they had to learn about the new technologies.

As these technologies took hold, it was, at first, a matter of getting familiar with them. But as they began to make profound changes in the way business worked, it was more and more a matter of striving to keep up with the rapid innovations—yet inevitably falling behind.

This was the business side of "times they are a-changing", and the changes amounted to a continuous shortening of both the business cycle and career longevity. Where in the past you might have had a career that fit entirely within a single technological generation, this was no longer the case. Thirty-year careers became 20-year careers, then 15-year careers. The technological generations have started to become shorter and shorter and will continue to shorten. Consequently, a career necessarily shifted and started to include several permutations. Businesses started to adapt to the idea that they would serve more than one consumer generation and face more than one generation of competitive players. More significantly, it would no longer be possible to stay on top by just relying on experience and hard-won knowledge. From now on, employees and leaders would have to learn continuously.

The objective now was not simply to direct the company and the organization; it was to somehow avoid obsolescence. For many, that effort would become pretty much impossible with the coming of the digital revolution. Changes began arriving in dizzying succession, the mastery of one being made useless by the arrival of the next.

The world is changing so rapidly today that if any small-to-medium-sized business or the CEO of any such organization remains in the same place for more than three years, by the end of that time, they'll be five years behind, and much of their hard-won knowledge and experience reduced to useless baggage.

But that's one of the more benign effects of the digital revolution. As we all know, the digital revolution is changing the very fabric of our lives, and there's no sign that the changing is over or even slowing down. Almost every week brings us new capabilities and new connections— with each other, with our work and with every imaginable electronic medium.

It's not just that more things have been invented, it's that more of them have become integrated and adopted. The changes have been universal, more standards-based. This has allowed people to concentrate on leveraging technology and combining it, not just on adopting it.

It's no big news that technology is changing society. But the implications of these changes are much less obvious, and their impact on the business environment is even more difficult to recognize. After all, it took us decades to truly understand the broad societal effects of the birth control pill, jet travel or even television. Similarly, we are just beginning to understand the impact the Internet has and will continue to have on our lives as individuals and on our society.

Generational Conflicts

Some aspects of this transformation, however, are slowly becoming clear. For instance, the pace of change has downgraded the value of experience and accumulated knowledge. This, in turn, has reduced the value of age and time in service. Grey hair is no longer a sign of competence and wisdom. In many circumstances, it gives young people the opposite impression.

This has given power to younger people that they never had before. It is their very youth that signals their technological currency and their understanding of 21st century society. They're the ones who have mastered today's popular culture and its language, both of which are essential to understanding the contemporary business environment.

This has had a huge impact on the relationship between the generations. Once upon a time, younger people looked up to older people in the work environment. This is less and less true. Younger people find themselves understanding more than their elders, not only about the technology but also about society itself. This inevitably undermines the authority of older leadership. It tends to flatten organizational hierarchies—at least in practice.

To the CEOs who have put in their time and risen to the top, who have slowly and with great effort achieved position and power, these younger people, all too often, look like poachers and upstarts. They're seen as rivals, not as resources. Obviously, this is not the best way to do business.

If the only major change in the last 30 years had been the new technologies, the 21st century would be significantly different from the 20th. But the new technologies have opened the door to sweeping social changes that are also having a profound impact on organizations of all kinds, and on the very foundations of the business world in practically every country on Earth.

One World

"The world is getting smaller", or so goes the old cliché, no doubt heard for the first time in 1902 when Marconi managed to transmit a wireless telegraph message across the Atlantic, from the Old World to the New. And that was before steamships and Lindbergh, and the Boeing 707 and Yuri Gagarin and all that followed. Now it's electrons and photons that are doing the shrinking, not atoms. There is now no distance between any two points on Earth, at least not in time.

As a result, American businesses interact in real time with Israeli businesses. Brazilian firms interact instantly with their Hong Kong suppliers. The Australian manufacturers of sheepskin coats communicate, with zero delay, with their Scandinavian distributors. Shipments and orders can be traced instantly and on a worldwide basis.

This is still rather remarkable, if for most of your business career, the only way to interact with foreign companies or foreign branch offices was through expensive long-distance phone lines or uncertain snail mail. But it's not so remarkable to those who are now entering executive ranks. They saw it coming. It's just more of what they're already used to. We have a world almost without borders, a world in which markets, production facilities, headquarters offices, sales forces and any other part of the organization can be almost anywhere.

This means that the whole world is open to you and your company. It also means that the whole world is open to your competitors. Few companies own a market purely on the basis of geography. Of course, this situation has been developing for some time, but now it is so easy to do business on a global basis that many small-and-medium-sized companies, which would have considered it well beyond their reach in earlier times, are finding themselves with global opportunities no matter where they're located.

Diversity with a Capital "D"

The electronic networks that connect us in almost every conceivable way have encouraged vast movements of people across the globe in many different directions.

This complicates life for the companies that expect their people to look the same, act the same and be the same. Employees are likely to come from very different backgrounds, and finding common values and norms is quite a challenge. The same is true of customers, not only for those companies that want to operate in global markets, but also for those who are concentrating on their home marketplace. That marketplace, too, is more multicultural than ever before, whether we're talking about America, Europe or Asia.

There's also been a rise in a different kind of diversity—a diversity characterized by differences in knowledge and interests, by behavioral differences and by differences in personal style. This diversity is a social phenomenon, the result of a mixture of generations, genders, cultural shifts and multiculturalism. And it's a dynamic diversity, since each of the elements within it is changing.

Today, any organization anywhere in the Western world is likely to have a payroll that includes people of different skin color, from different religious backgrounds, new immigrants and third-generation citizens, new college graduates, people without high school degrees, single mothers, grandmothers, older people looking for new careers, geeks who spend their off-hours in cyberspace, people who wear jeans and T-shirts to symphony orchestra performances, folk who don't drink, dance or party, people impatient for retirement, people afraid of retirement, moderates, liberals and conservatives, and people from every kind of fringe—social, political, sexual and psychological.

It's almost as though every company has been allocated a scientifically selected and mathematically valid sample—continuously changing—of the entire international population. The result is anything but your father's corporation. It is something new in the history of humankind.

Diversity at this level greatly complicates corporate management, because it means that 20th century employment standards—racial, religious, language, educational, age and gender—no longer apply. The 21st century organization must run according to a much more flexible set of rules and expectations. In these circumstances, individuality becomes an extremely powerful force, smothered only at great risk.

There are enormous advantages to diversity, especially diversity and individuality that is encouraged and respected. It results in a hybridization of thought and action, the joining of many different strands together. And like crop hybrids, the hybrid workforce is stronger, more vital, and more resistant to pests than its purebred counterpart.

The Changing Customer

Just as the workforce has been transformed in the last 30 years, so has the marketplace—more so, if that is possible. Multiculturalism and the opening of global markets have created customer bases that are stunningly diverse.

In the 21st century, it's no longer enough simply to offer goods and services. Companies must now take into account their customers' different nationalities, religions, cultures, languages, customs—not to mention competition from every direction, close by and far away.

Not only are today's customers more diverse, they are intrinsically different from yesterday's. Competition was less intense in the 20th century, and customers were more likely to buy, unquestioningly, whatever goods and services they were offered. They didn't have very many choices and were grateful for what the market brought them. The supplier was in charge of the relationship, to the extent that a relationship existed.

Today's customers are much too well informed for that. They frequently know as much about the marketplace as the companies who serve it. They know their choices. They know what they have to pay. They know what they should be getting. This applies not only to physical products and specific services, but also to the way these goods and services are delivered, and to the relationship customers will have with their supplier, before the sale, during the sale and especially after the sale. Customers may be buying the goods and services, but the suppliers are buying, or trying to buy their customers' loyalty. Looking for new customers is expensive.

Today's customers are demanding, like never before. They want what they want, and that isn't enough. They want more. They want new and then newer, and they want it fast. They want their purchase to fit them like a glove, to match their external needs and their inner desires, even if they're unaware of them. They want it customized, personalized and individualized.

Today's customers judge their supplier not just on the quality of the goods or services provided, but on the totality of their experience as well. That includes the product or service, customer service, the attitude of everyone in the company who comes into contact with the customers, the economic, social and even political values of the company and its products, and last, but not least, the ease of doing business.

Bottom line: perfection may be impossible, but good enough is no longer good enough. Suppliers that expect to keep their customers had better exceed expectations in every contact.

Other Changes

Some of the changes of the last 30 years have more to do with corporations and other organizations than with the rest of society. For instance, in recent years, there has been a clear trend towards horizontal cooperation between organizations (as opposed to vertical cooperation). This is blurring the once sharp line between competition and cooperation. It has created what once would have been unlikely alliances, with benefits for both parties. Co-opetition has become a viable and legitimate strategy.

In addition, capital markets have begun to change their standards for judging and evaluating companies. In the past, current net value was the only central criterion. Now, analysts are looking more deeply, not only at companies' present value, but on potential future performance, based on the character, ambitions and foresightedness of company CEOs and other leaders. Intangible assets are now creating even more value for companies than the bricks and mortar of the traditional Profit & Loss.

In this brief analysis, we've described how the 21st century business environment is different from its 20th century counterpart. We've talked about some truly fundamental changes—technological changes, globalism, multiculturalism, the diversity explosion and the empowered consumer.

When you take all of these factors together, this is not just change. It is transformation. We are living in a different world than we were 30 years ago, or even ten years ago. But it may not look or feel that way, in part because the changes, fundamental as they are, are not happening everywhere with the same speed. Or, as science-fiction writer William Gibson once said, "The future is here. It's just not evenly distributed yet."

As fast as the world is changing, it is surprising how most of the world doesn't realize the significance of these changes. Many of today's CEOs are still trying to repeat the successes they had 20 years ago, or those of their predecessors, by doing what worked then. What they can't know is how their predecessors would have behaved in this new world.

At the outer edge, there are CEOs who have gained a profound understanding of the world in which they live. But they are facing toward the future—not so much to anticipate it, but to create it. These are the people with the best chance of success in this new world.

Part Three: The Transorganization (2003 to-date)

Change alone is eternal, perpetual, immortal.
Arthur Schopenhauer

Out of all the profound changes of the last few decades, a new kind of organization has emerged, an organization distinctly different from those that came before it. We call it the T-Organization, or transorganization.

Transorganizations are organizations in a state of permanent transformation. They are not just gradually changing through incremental improvement, but are forever redefining their core business and their potential areas of growth, and with greater speed than ever.

Most P-Organizations are just beginning to recognize the need to change. Fully-fledged T-Organizations are still relatively few in number. But they are the harbingers of the future, beginning to appear throughout the world, and in some very unexpected places: a supermarket chain company in New York, a holding company in Brazil, or a manufacturer of a semiconductor machinery in Israel, for example.

What are the major characteristics of transorganizations? We claim they are the following and we will look at each of these characteristics in turn:

- They shape their strategy and leadership via a special prism—their soul.
- They act humanistically, not mechanistically.
- They look differently at "organizational structure".
- They have co-action culture.
- They excel in distance-based operations.
- They master flexibility as a core virtue.
- They look for competences externally.
- They de-emphasize power and focus on energy.
- They produce "offerings".
- They manage experation-based operations.
- They speak a different language.
- They overcome the challenge of over-communications.

The Soul of the Transorganization

Perhaps the most profound difference between traditional companies and transorganizations is that the transorganization has consciously identified and shaped its *soul*; by that we mean the intrinsic corporate identity that underlies all that it does, that informs its business practices, its aims and goals, its internal and external relationships and its intangible sense of direction—shared in an aligned way between its employees, its managers, its shareholders and its business partners.

This should not be confused with the superficial image that conventional corporations present to their customers, their suppliers and the outside world, through advertising, public relations and the public appearances of the CEO. This image is an aspect of marketing, not a proclamation of inner identity.

For transorganizations, understanding and developing the soul is a highly conscious and intentional process. It is their reason for being, their interface with the world. It is why they do what they do, in the manner they do.

What are the elements in the soul of the transorganization? There are many, and they vary in strength and in combination. Does the company see itself as a technological leader or a market leader? Is it satisfied to be a niche player? Does it seek market share above all else? How does it see its social responsibilities? How does it feel about its customers, its employees, and its competitors? How big does it want to get?

The best way to describe the soul is through the metaphor of a "prism". On the following page is a diagram of the six angles—or dimensions—of that prism:

The Transorganization's Prism of the Soul

Brand Identity

Knowledge Management

Sensors & Information Flow—

Your Biz

Financial Awareness

Collective Stakeholders' Experience

Core Business Clarity

1. Core Business Clarity is perhaps the most fundamental element of any transorganization's soul. The simple answer to the question "what business are we in?" is no longer sufficient, because it looks at the past rather than the future. Instead, transorganizations ask, "what business do we want to be, and what business do we want to build?" It is surprising how many organizations have not answered these tough questions. Many businesses we know simply continue "to do what they are best at" (ignoring that those markets might disappear). Transorganizations should keep asking this question from time to time—as they are constantly re-shaping their future.

2. Collective Stakeholders' Experience. Transorganizations do not define their soul from "their cave" but care about the experience that they generate; and they keep asking the question "what is the experience that we want to generate?" rather than just measuring where they are. Stakeholders' Experience Management is a tough task yet its continuous development builds the transorganization's soul.

3. Financial Awareness. Real-time awareness of the transorganization's financial health and well-being is too often ignored. The need to have real-time awareness of

financial health and risks is far from being acted upon, and it is not just a question of "information systems". The balance between profit awareness and proper investments is just one example of what we mean by financial health. Is "profit today"—rather than "investment for growth tomorrow"—the right value? This is just one aspect of the financial dimension of the transorganization soul. And clearly, financial awareness requires sophisticated real-time sensors in order to build a healthy, real time, accurate and meaningful financial awareness.

4. Sensors and Information Flow. In an era where organizations are inundated with huge amounts of data, there is a need to understand what's relevant. The information transorganizations choose to follow, accumulate, process and disseminate is filtered by their soul, and it is surprising to see how many organizations are collecting tons of data without first asking what's really relevant.

5. Knowledge Management. The soul of transorganizations shapes the way they learn, accumulate knowledge, store, disseminate and discard knowledge. In the era of the short life cycle of knowledge, the soul of the organization filters, shapes and determines the process of knowledge accumulation and management. Again we are surprised to see how many organizations are missing the importance of building effective knowledge management practice. There is a need to track, scale and develop both the tacit and experiential knowledge in an organization.

6. Brand Identity. Last but not least, brand identity is shaped by the soul of the organization, and not vice versa... when it is aligned with the soul—people recognize that the brand identity is genuine; if it is not—they will easily see through it and will not "buy" the projected identity. Therefore, it is imperative that once transorganizations reflect and define their soul, they should resort to re-branding.

The above six dimensions are the angles of the transorganization's prism through which the transorganization sees its soul. They determine the quality of its products and services. They determine its marketing philosophy. They determine the nature of the working environment. They inform its public behavior and the manner in which it exercises its citizenship. They are embedded in everything the transorganization does.

In fact, in order to reach this level of awareness, the transorganization needs an on-going source of energy that will become the light illuminating this prism. And that's one of the new responsibilities of the leaders of transorganizations, who will be described later in the book.

Humanistic vs. mechanistic

Another striking difference between transorganizations and traditional organizations is that transorganizations consciously operate humanistically rather than mechanically.

It's tempting to regard this with cynicism, as if were just another New Age bumper sticker. It is anything but that. It is real, it is practical and it's directed at the bottom line, at survival and success.

Transorganizations are less concerned about fitting people into jobs than they are about fitting jobs to the people. They don't put permanent and limiting labels on people, like "numbers guy" or "technology guy" or "production guy". They provide opportunities for personal and professional development and they reward changes and improvements. They encourage growth, additional education, new interests.

Of course transorganizations hire people for their skill sets, in part, but they look at them much more deeply, at their preferences, inclinations, talents, weaknesses, capacities, personal motivations, intellectual lives, and emotional lives, all of which govern their behavior and their attitudes toward themselves and their place in the company, in the working world and in life.

That means transorganizations recognize and respect the fact that all of their employees have rich, meaningful, and important second lives, lives filled with families, recreation, hobbies, interests, concerns, beliefs— lives that are of transcendent importance to them. Transorganizations understand that fulfilling second lives make their employees more capable and more valuable. Recognition of employees' second lives is reflected in the job, through attitudes, benefits and consideration.

Employees are not a nameless, faceless herd, but distinct individuals with distinct qualifications, needs and situations. They work *with* others more than they work *for* others.

The working atmosphere at a transorganization is distinctly different from previous organizational iterations. It is easy, friendly, unceremonious and less formal in every way—in attire, meetings, titles and names, hours, protocol and other traditional rules.

Within the transorganization, at any given time, some people—and it could be just about anyone—will not be working in a traditional setting. They're at home or on the road, working on their own or connecting with others, as necessary, electronically. They are not chained to their desks either figuratively or literally.

New ways of structuring the organization

In our consulting work, we often ask people how they designed their organizations—what was their guiding principle, other than division of responsibility, accountability, span of control, business lines, etc. The typical answer: by "functions". And when we ask how their people truly interact, the answer is by "problems" or "tasks". So we ask, "Who is your Vice President for non-paying customers?" Or "Who is your director for non-functioning products?" And "Who is running your department of always-late new products?" And "Who is the Vice President of unhappy customers?"

CEOs and other leaders tend to design organizations based on "ideal and positive" functions—collection, product quality, research and development and customer care. But this structure does not really reflect organizational needs today.

Why? Because whenever an organization faces a *real* challenge, it needs to involve several departments and people from different disciplines. So, in fact, the current "physical" structure—the organizational hierarchy—is mainly a reservoir of talent and expertise. The "borders" between departments in a transorganization do not necessarily mark a clear allocation of ownership, responsiveness and problem-solving responsibility.

We saw this clearly at one company we were advising. It was having a problem with a major customer concerning delayed payment. It had regular procedures to deal with this kind of problem, but these procedures had failed. We urged them to assemble a task force that included people from sales, customer care, operations, legal and finance and assigned the problem to this group.

It wasn't easy for the organization to do this. It wasn't the way it normally operated. It was difficult to cross-departmental boundaries, difficult to identify which person—from which department—might be helpful. The initial meeting was awkward. It was hard for everyone to articulate and share a complete, 360-degree view of the customer's situation. Then someone made a suggestion, someone who wasn't expected to contribute much, someone from a department that was peripherally involved at best. Within 24 hours, the problem was solved.

In a transorganization, this approach is built-in; it is legitimate and spontaneous. Transorganizations habitually create ad-hoc task forces, coalitions of expertise from several different domains. And they easily put together different teams from different departments to deal with different kinds of challenges, as appropriate.

Thus, transorganizations have fundamental differences from traditional organizations even in their basic structure. Instead of being built according to strongly hierarchical organization charts, the charts of transorganizations are remarkably flat and intensively networked. Many layers have been cut out of the usual "chain of command", so that more people have direct contact with higher-level officers. This gives new ideas easier, faster access to the top, and it gives leaders easier, faster access to the people below them— the people whose hearts and minds they must win over in order to mobilize the organization's vision and goals.

Ideally, transorganizations are shaped like amoebas, not high-rise buildings. They change shape as necessary, one nodule expanding, another shrinking, two nodules moving closer together or further apart, as necessary, and always in flux. The object is connected flexibility, not rigid structure.

To use a computer metaphor, the transorganization consists of a group of network hubs, not a mainframe and a series of nodes. It is not a pyramid, but an expanding series of interconnecting roads.

What's the value of this less-structured structure?

The main advantage is flexibility. Transorganizations are able to deal with challenges that impinge on two or more conventional departments without having to rewrite the organization chart every time circumstances change.

Operating with an amoeba-like structure and with semi-permeable borders, transorganizations can easily form cross-departmental teams to work on multidisciplinary problems or opportunities, then to change course and form new cross-departmental teams as the challenges change, or as new challenges develop.

In these transorganizations, departments may still exist, at least in name, but they are less formal and less constrained. They do not operate separately, but with knowledge of each other, and emigration and immigration from one department to another is not against the rules, but encouraged when it makes sense for everyone.

This allows personnel and expertise to be deployed in an ad hoc, task-oriented manner that meets the dynamic needs of the transorganization and leverages the human talent available. It allows for the natural emergence of a dynamic self-organizing procedure, in which people from a number of different departments become aware of a problem or spot an opportunity and voluntarily assemble themselves into a team to deal with it.

There is a price to pay for creating this kind of transorganizational structure, and it's the executives and managers who will have to pay it. Flattening the organization chart involves the re-allocation of the tangible managerial assets such as people, budgets, span of control, etc.

This may well cause anguish among the executives whose titles have been shortened, whose position in the organization chart has just gone down a level, who have trouble accepting the need to share resources, who are accustomed to having a large number of people report to them, etc. They will feel, often acutely, a loss of status and power. But as we shall see, the words "status" and "power" belong to previous organizational ages.

Flattening the organization presents a serious management challenge—how to shift from the status and power view of highly structured organizations to the task-driven and amoeba-shaped structure of the transorganization. Leaders of transorganizations need to find ways to model, drive and reward entrepreneurial behavior that focuses on cross-department coalitions, and ways to develop and encourage the formation of brilliant, unstructured ad hoc teams spontaneously appearing out of the amoeba-like shape of the transorganization.

We are not suggesting the elimination of all structure and organization. The charts are still necessary, but the rigidity of the past cannot continue.

Co-Action Culture

"We have a major problem", said a friend of ours, an executive in the R&D section of one of the largest high-tech companies. "Our veteran researchers and scientists are having trouble with our new researchers and scientists. They feel their authority isn't being respected and they're not being taken seriously. The new people are accusing the old people of being masters of 'old think,' and not being up to date. One of our most brilliant new hires has told me he doesn't understand what value he's getting from his experienced manager."

We recommended that he speak to his managers about the need to develop the necessary skills to deal with people who may know more than they do, instead of assuming the people they're managing know less than they do and are dependent on their expertise. We could see that life experience, managerial maturity, emotional intelligence skills, judgment capability, asking the right questions, and radiating a positive personality were as important, if not more important, than pure domain expertise. Building a creative atmosphere that will inspire innovation is sometimes as difficult as inventing new technology.

For hundreds of years, the Western world operated on the conviction that knowledge and expertise—as well as age—were the key factors in appointing people to managerial positions. The best shift manager became the line manager, and the best line manager became the factory manager, etc. The concept was both simple and reasonable: the more you knew, the better a manager you would make. And this idea has survived to this day. Many organizations still hold these views, especially those with a clear hierarchical structure and a reasonably routine and stable working situation. The idea that performance and knowledge should lead to promotion is still deeply rooted in the industrial environment. But corporations rarely look for a third quality, one that could be far more important than the other two: the ability to cope with the unknown and the unexpected.

Transorganizations recognize that a fundamental change is taking place in the old "knowledge age" archetype. And this change has altered the way they address problems and challenges—and even how they make promotions.

In the knowledge age, the experienced veterans and managers taught newcomers and showed them how to solve problems. It was quite easy to map out problems and solutions, and when an "unknown" problem popped up, it was turned over to experts, who figured out the solution and taught it to the rest of the organization. This "internship" model still applies to many professions and working environments that are the least affected by social, technological and economic changes.

The implications of this model are very interesting:

- The experts become the heroes of the corporation.
- There is a growing need for specialization, to build deeper expertise.
- The organization functions best when problems are routed to those who can solve them.

The equation is clear: experience equals value. But that is the old equation. The new equation is not so neat, but more in tune with today's realities. We call it the "meta-knowledge" equation.

Meta-knowledge is not the know-how needed to solve a problem. It is the know-how needed to assemble the resources necessary to solve a problem. It is the difference between knowing that the population of Zambia is 11,668,000 and knowing how to find that information. Meta-knowledge involves the ability to find or assemble information from external sources, such as Google, or books, or experts, and most importantly, it is the art of harnessing collective intelligence in order to solve problems and challenges. In a way, it requires a once brilliant violinist to become a successful conductor.

Today's organizations face such complex problems, and in such numbers, that mere knowledge doesn't help much. It is insufficient. Meta-knowledge is needed to identify (and assemble) the team that has the resources necessary to solve the problem. The complexity of the problems is such that single hierarchical departments very frequently do not possess the knowledge resources required to efficiently come up with solutions.

This may sound like nothing more than a "routing" exercise, but that's an enormous over-simplification. The responsible person must map the knowledge gaps in their team and quickly identify personnel who "own" the required know-how. Then, he or she must form an ad-hoc coalition to tackle the problem.

But who determines what problems need to be addressed this way? Who forms the coalitions, and based on what priorities? The answers to these questions, we believe, are at the core of organizational success in the 21st century. In the past, it might have seemed that the answer was more *command and control*, the traditional ways for a CEO to motivate and direct his team. But the meta-knowledge age demands something else, something very different. People who are clear about their organization's priorities and vision will be able to find solutions through self-organizing, through the opposite of command and control and we call this—*collaborate and enrol.*

We know that every organization is full of talent islands that are not being put to work, simply because employees are measured by traditional standards—their production and their accomplishments within their departments. This does not encourage self-organization or freedom of initiative, and it short-circuits employee creativity and resourcefulness.

It is the 'co-action culture' of the transorganization that avoids these pitfalls. And we're not simply talking about a skill. We're talking about a way of working, a business and social system in which everyone in the company participates, a world where the idea of "roles and responsibilities" has been replaced by "multidisciplinary rules, responsibilities and networked interactions".

We believe that transorganizations in complex industries or industries that offer complex products or services—the entire high-tech sector, for instance—should devote at least 10% of their productive labor time to cross-departmental, co-action activities. The leadership should not only welcome and endorse this, it should identify areas that would benefit from more co-action and measure and monitor initiatives that facilitate it.

In transorganizations with a healthy co-action culture, traditional performance-based compensation—by itself—is too simple and potentially unfair. Other factors have to be added in, especially cross-departmental initiatives and overall company performance.

The co-action culture also has an impact on a transorganization's assessment of its organizational and human capital, and on its recruiting criteria. So they rate their people according to their participation in and attitude toward co-action activities, and they seek people who are comfortable in this kind of environment.

By cutting back on command and control, and encouraging the organization and its people to adapt to the new culture, transorganizations have found that resourceful members of its team will self-organize, building coalitions in order to quickly respond and act.

We saw a good real-life example of this in one of the companies we consulted with. One of the R&D managers insisted that his engineers visit customer sites with the service engineers. He said he wanted the academic types to see what the service people were doing and vice versa, in the hopes that this would lead to more efficient problem solving. This approach yielded three benefits. First, it eliminated the endemic finger-pointing between the two groups. They stopped seeing themselves as "us" and "them". Second, the R&D people proved very helpful with customer problems, solving them in a creative and useful manner. Third, by learning more about product problems and issues from the service engineers, the R&D people became motivated to solve these problems in future product generations.

Another company we worked with was in the midst of a crisis. They had lost a lot of business to competitors. So, a weekly forum was created, bringing together sales people, R&D scientists, marketing and operations people for three hours to talk about key prospects and key deals.

This forum generated amazing energy. All the participants realized it was up to them to jointly address the company's problems, share their insights and propose solutions. We heard sales executives coming up with technical solutions, and operations people providing salespeople with great tips on how to deal with a complex sales situation.

This interaction so energized the company that within six months it had pulled itself out of the ditch and was experiencing solid growth. The company continues to hold the weekly forums years after that crisis.

Distance-Based Operations

Ideally, transorganizations have no borders. They are communities of people who may be physically distant from each other. This may sound like organizations of the past, with many locations, connected and managed with the same approach, but the difference is profound. Transorganizations are everywhere. Employees and executives are working from a distance. They interact with each other from the road, from home, from vacation resorts (unfortunately…) and, with the rise of amoeba-shaped functionality, there may be long periods in which managers rarely see their team members face-to-face.

We believe that this trend is still at its beginnings. In the coming years, it will accelerate, driven by the need to save on transportation costs (both for financial and global sustainability reasons) and the need to limit productivity losses caused by lengthening commuting times, and empowered by mobile videoconferencing and other easy-to-use forms of digital communication. As a result, more people will be going to work without changing their physical environment, and working together without being together. Transorganizations are reacting to this change by allowing a higher and higher degree of flexible time management, even though that will require two major shifts in behavior:

- Leaders will have to move from the conventional "hands-on", "face-to-face" presence that exerts authority and controls and models behavior, toward an awareness-based presence that will persist even if the leader isn't face-to-face with his people. In other words, leaders will have to learn how to create an impact from a distance, a skill that we will discuss elsewhere in the book.

- Leaders will have to shift from the traditional model of measuring effort and results to measuring results, co-action and impact. The location-based workplace enabled a clear measurement of time spent on the job, translated into an "effort" measurement, but distance-based operations will not allow that. Instead, performance appraisals should look at "results and meeting objectives". And leaders will have to develop trust schemes to help them assess the value of their people's contributions.

We've talked to many managers who've found it hard to cope with the physical absence of their team members. They felt proximity and presence was essential not just so they could control their people, but so they could influence them and assess their performance. "If an employee isn't here", we often heard, "I don't know where he is and what he is doing". This apparent loss of control, as well as the sense of togetherness, was a difficult hurdle for many managers. Yet it is evidence of something more challenging—a lack of trust.

The transorganizations that have already shifted away from this view have a competitive edge in attracting new talent. Upcoming generations are quite confident that they can stay connected and intimately interact even if they are not within eyeshot.

In addition, this kind of organizational flexibility enables improved productivity for freethinking, fast-moving employees, to whom self-fulfillment is at least as important as success on the job.

A Question of Competence

In the past, organizations were self-contained and self-sufficient. If a skill was perceived as crucial, the organization had to own it. One result of this was the age of specialization and the age of professionalism—two of the greatest accomplishments of S-Organizations and P-Organizations.

Today, however, it can be difficult to develop internally the expertise necessary to succeed and deliver quality performance. For example, the complexity of manufacturing might be too challenging for SMB companies to address and they are much better off outsourcing their manufacturing to a third-party manufacturing operation, which has the required expertise and economies of scale. The same applies, for example, to marketing skills—if you need the brilliance and graphic capabilities of top designers, it is sometimes easier to outsource these marketing tasks to a marketing company rather than doing it in-house (also, top marketing talents will more likely work for a specialty marketing shop because it can offer them diverse projects which require their creativity and innovation again and again, while working for an SMB might be too "limiting"). So transorganizations do not (and should not) own all the skills they need. They acquire the skills and expertise they need from other, trusted external parties.

This approach requires a continuous rethinking of a basic question: "What really is the transorganization's 'core competence'?" To answer this question, transorganizations must consider several factors.

- Transorganizations need to balance two different impulses: 1) the desire to provide more and more value to customers and to provide wider and more flexible offerings, in order to meet customers' expectations; and 2) the urge not to own competencies that aren't necessary, that are costly to maintain and are a drain on overall efficiency. Whether in manufacturing or marketing tasks, transorganizations resort to more and more outsourcing practices in order to focus on their core competencies.

- It's not easy to find outside competence on demand, in real time. That requires close management of the "competency marketplaces", making sure the organization has rapid access to many different external pools of talent and has the ability to quickly identify, contract and engage the skills it needs. The objective is to develop a network of potential providers and skills and competence, ready to be supplied on-demand, in real time, by people and organizations acting as strategic partners. These could be in almost any business area: R&D, marketing, financial, legal and operations resources.

- When bringing in external competencies, transorganizations should realize that fulfilling their mission and their vision is heavily dependent on "others". That means it is essential that these "others" are engaged with the transorganization's vision, mission and strategy. This is especially important as the border between the transorganization and its "others" begins to fade away, which is what happens with frequent engagement. This requires two shifts in behavior; being sensitive to the "others'" diversity, and being able to trust "others" and share with them the transorganization's soul.

- On occasion, a "contractible on-demand competency" may suddenly become a "must-own competence" for the transorganization. A typical example of this is when a company transforms its "to go to market" strategy from an indirect product distribution model to a direct sales model. At this point, the outside organizations that once acted as distributors may now be needed as internal employees. This can be challenging, since the transorganization is asking people who were once outside partners to give up the ownership of their enterprises and to become employees. This requires M&A operations at a very high level of sensitivity.

When all of these elements are combined, the transorganization becomes the nucleus of a successful network of organizations, sharing a common purpose and working together to ensure their mutual growth and success. This interdependency may create unconventional models of commerce and exchange, models based on risk and reward sharing, on economy of scale and performance-based payments. And that could lead to cooperation with and between external entities that compete with each other, everyone basing their actions on trust and shared responsibility, not fear and concern.

In general, the leaders of traditional corporations do not have a clear view of their partner networks and they don't feel any need to share their vision and strategies with these external suppliers. This will put them at a serious disadvantage against transorganizations that have mastered the art of cooperating with external partners, the art of friendly in-sourcing and acquisition and the art of friendly outsourcing.

Energy-Based Management

Here's a situation that had us puzzled when we first heard about it. One of the companies for which we consulted had launched half a dozen projects based on innovative ideas, with the intent of turning some of them into new business lines. All of them seemed destined for success when initiated. But by the time we were called in, roughly two years later, some of the once promising initiatives had either been closed down or were on the verge of failure. Even more puzzling, several other projects, deemed more risky at the time, were turning into surprising successes.

The company, naturally anxious to avoid further errors of this kind and still hoping to rescue some of the projects, asked us to figure out why the promising projects had failed and the dubious ones had succeeded. "We just don't understand what happened", they said. "All of the projects had comparable staffs, all of them had similar working operations, the managers all came from the top of the line and the goal was the same: create new growth engines for the company. Why were the results so different?"

We looked at these projects and received permission to sit in—quietly—at each team's weekly project meetings. It took just one complete cycle of meetings to figure out what had happened. *Energetic* leaders drove the successful projects, while *powerful* leaders ran the problematic projects.

The differences were obvious. The powerful leaders had established hierarchies, parceled out responsibilities and started giving out orders.

The energetic leaders did not command. They enabled positive behavior. They encouraged people to become entrepreneurs. They allowed people to seek external advice. They treated their team with empathy, accepting small failures and mistakes, encouraging their people to take risks.

Transorganizations, with their flat structure and shared leadership, are naturally suited to de-emphasize power and focus on energy. In fact, we believe that sensing, measuring, building and replenishing energy is crucial to corporate success. But herein lies a problem: how can organizations tell when they don't have enough of it? And how can they manage it?

Transorganizations can spot energy levels in individuals and organizations by looking at a number of criteria: optimism, drive, imagination, positive language, willingness to take risks, teamwork, confidence, physical and mental health, adaptability, initiative, working-to-production hours ratio, clarity of purpose, and, most of all, harmony with the organization's soul, with its vision and goals.

And there are some other, more complex factors to consider when evaluating organizational and individual energy as well:

- First, organizations should look at the way they're treating errors. Are they handled and analyzed in the "execution space" or in the "education space"? Are errors—within reason—used as a way to increase performance through education and a positive learning cycle or are they used to deter people from taking risks and initiatives? Empathy toward errors—using errors as an opportunity to learn and develop—is a good sign that the organization has the energy it needs to pursue its goals.

- Second, organizations should examine the bursts of energy that come from individuals and groups. Are these examples of balanced enthusiasm or overheated passion? The first is good, the second may not be. Overly passionate people can be threatening to other people, at the peer, subordinate or managerial level. So it is important to develop the ability to distinguish between healthy, simple and authentic enthusiasm (energy...) and exaggerated, out-of-proportion obsession for results, success and recognition (power...).

- Third, organizations should look at their level of internal entrepreneurship. The companies that allow a higher degree of initiative and entrepreneurship are energy-driven and they are creating strong pools of energy. Another indicator: the mobilization of ideas and the free movement of people between departments.

Transorganizations use their awareness of these qualities to evaluate and deploy personnel according to their energy levels rather than their seniority or title. And they consciously work to raise everyone's energy level. For example, they try to avoid hiring people with a high degree of negativity, because negativity drains energy. They also discourage frequent meetings, for the same reason.

In addition, a great deal of organizational energy is wasted on hidden issues such as turf battles, rivalries, slights (real and imagined), perceptions of unfairness, credit or blame apparently improperly assigned, etc. The weapon transorganizations employ against energy drains of this kind is truth telling. The idea is to make the invisible visible, so that it can be dealt with.

Within the transorganization, truth telling is just an extension of openness, honesty and respect for their people. It is a way to leverage the CEO's search for reality so that its benefits can impact the entire organization.

Establishing a pervasive atmosphere of honesty within an organization is very difficult, since employees often feel they need to lie or conceal in order to protect themselves. One way to deal with this is to put a high premium on truth, no matter how painful it may be, and to reward it.

Flexibility as a Core Virtue

One of the transorganization's most prominent characteristics is flexibility. It's something they strive for at every level, beginning with recruitment. They look for people who are naturally open, fast and flexible, who are temperamentally in sync with the organization's attitudes and goals, with its soul.

The objective is to create an organization in which the proper mind-set need not be imposed on employees from the top down, but instead reflects the genuine character and inclinations of its people, that harmony exists from top to bottom and from bottom to top, at the soul level.

For example, if a basketball team's coach is naturally more focused on defense than on offense, the team will do better and he will do better if he builds a unit whose individual members have the same inclinations. The same goes for transorganizations.

And hiring the people who appear to be right for the company isn't the end of it. Transorganizations need to look at their people, new hires and veterans alike, and continually evaluate them on the basis of their performance in teams and their ability to effectively collaborate with others. Just as they ask their people to be flexible, transorganizations strive to be flexible themselves. Broadly speaking, they certainly have clear goals, but they are continually re-evaluating those goals, treating them not as fixed points at which they can arrive, once and for all, but as moving targets. The result is that transorganizations constantly transform themselves, redefining the meaning of success, and raising the bar.

What do Transorganizations Generate?

Conventional organizations make products or deliver services. Transorganizations do much more. They generate *offerings*. What's the difference? Products are stand-alone items, sent out in boxes or put on shelves and purchased by customers who scarcely connect them to their manufacturers.

Offerings retain their connection to the corporation indefinitely and they link the corporation to the customer for as long as they last. The transorganization's intent is that their products help create a bond between them and their customers, a lasting relationship that, over time, will deliver more products to the customer and lead him to see the organization as an essential resource.

Offerings are different from products in yet another way. They are more tentative. A product is what it is and customers can take it or leave it. An offering is a kind of on-going experiment. It's an effort to meet or exceed customer expectations, or provide something customers didn't even know they wanted or needed until they saw it.

Making an offering, rather than just a product, requires organizations to attain a deep (and real-time) understanding of their customers and potential customers. It's not enough to collect data about their buying habits. Transorganizations delve deeper, into every aspect of their customers' lives. Their aim is to know their customers better, as well as the customers know themselves: to know the expectations of their customers, of which their customers themselves are only dimly aware, if at all.

A very vivid example of this came through watching a business develop over a period of more than 40 years. A craftsman and an expert in book binding, a very competitive business at the time, had a very different way of doing business—his small bookbinding shop became a meeting place for people, where he would host people for a chat, serving drinks and cakes. Working became a social experience, beyond a customer-supplier relationship. Furthermore, he made a special effort to deliver the legal books, which he had restored and bound, to his customers' offices or even their homes (where, by the way, he would always spot more books which needed restoration...). He charged the highest prices in town, yet more and more people chose to work with him simply because of the quality of the whole experience and the convenience.

And all of that was done for one reason: to bind more books.

Experations-Based Operations

In the past, organizations judged their operational effectiveness by internal measurement. Transorganizations have a different focus. They measure how their customers evaluate them, a recognition of the power shift from producer to consumer.

When making an offering, transorganizations go beyond guesswork, collected data and focus groups. They are passionate about understanding the *"experations"*—they ask customers to define their *expectations* of the *operations* and the offering, and they measure the customer's experience to modify the way they operate. They talk to their customers during and after the entire process of coming to market. And they listen. Thus, they increase the chance that their offering will survive in the marketplace.

Transorganizations also apply this knowledge to all the other contacts they may have with customers, no matter how brief or intangible. This includes advertising, sales and marketing efforts, product delivery, points of sale, help lines, complaint management, other telephone contacts, recalls, warranty service, parts returns and replacement, as well as its public behavior.

Organizations today touch their customers in many ways—face-to-face, over the phone, through a contact center, in exhibitions, on websites, through mail campaigns and many other points of interaction. And their customers judge them not just on how they perform at one point of interaction, but on the totality of their experiences—including the experience they have with the organization's product, service, attitude, values and the ease of doing business with it.

If you've ever wondered why companies that make "inferior" products, as defined by technical progress, sometimes do better in the marketplace than companies with obviously better products (think Beta vs. VHS), the reason is simple: customers do not just make their purchases solely on the product's capabilities. They make decisions on the basis of their whole experience with a company's *experations*.

One example of this is ease of doing business or EODB. Companies making the best product on the market, but burdening it with a mind-blowing process of configuring, ordering and pricing, will be rejected by customers who expect elegance, speed and simplicity when choosing products.

We've seen this personally, at a software company whose products were technically superior to those of the competition. Some potential customers nevertheless preferred the competition's products. We studied the problem and found that some customers felt their total experience with the competition was more satisfying. So the company we were advising improved its customer service and customer interaction model. They also formed an "Executive Council" and invited the executives of their top customers to serve as an advisory board. Consequently, the company simplified its delivery logistics and order management, as well as its professional service practices—and increased its market share. And it also became highly visible thanks to its contacts with the senior executives of its customers, tapping into many more strategic projects with much higher profiles.

It is striking to hear so many executives talking about their latest performance management system, which almost always involves internal measurements of some kind. And it is also striking to hear executives fighting back when confronted with the results of customer surveys or focus groups. They find it hard to believe that successful results for internal operations and performance measurements are, nonetheless, considered unacceptable by their relevant customers.

Too often, executives deal with this contradictory information by blaming their customers. "We had the best scores in customer service last year, but were surprised to see that customer loyalty has gone down. We're at a loss about what to do to retain customers."

Transorganizations meet the "experations" challenge in two ways.

First, they design a series of diverse touch point and interaction points in order to match customer expectations, both in the virtual digital world and in the physical, face-to-face touch point. The purpose is to create a unique business and human experience, which, if repeated, builds customer loyalty. Secondly, they adopt a holistic view of customer experience, throughout the customer life cycle. Thus, a bank branch manager will be able to understand what the customer experienced at the bank's online website recently, or what the contact center agent told the customer in their last phone conversation, so that he (or she) can deal with the customer knowledgeably and with sensitivity.

The Language of the Transorganization

Words matter. Language sets thinking, action and behavior. So it is interesting to note that in the transorganization, the daily working language of its employees has been affected by its new ways of doing business and by the new world in which it exists.

This new language is, in itself, transformative—so long as all the stakeholders in the organization—the leaders, employees, corporate branding, corporate communications—authentically adopt it, use it, and behave accordingly.

It's not that the old buzzwords have disappeared—or should disappear. The functional language of the P-Organizations still revolves around P-words: product, pricing, promotion, placement, profiling, positioning and profitability. These still drive many organizations and go a long way toward dictating their mindsets, their actions and their decisions. Many of these ways of thinking have contributed and continue to be key factors in organizational success.

But the sea changes of the 21st century have brought a new emphasis, another set of words of which many, by another happy coincidence, begin with the letter "C", far beyond the "Customer-driven" or "Customer focus" lingo.

- **Conversation**. We have often asked sales people about the prospects they are about to meet. What do people say about this prospect? What are the hot topics debated at this prospect's coffee corner or water cooler? What's on the prospect's mind today? The answers to these questions are key to the sales person's ability to shape his or her pitch and manage the conversation with the prospect. Most of the sales people we talked to couldn't answer these questions. On the other hand, other sales people spent hours preparing themselves for what would be a 20-minute conversation with their prospect, reading every piece of news about the prospect that they could find. You can easily guess which sales people were more successful.

- **Culture**. For the companies that want to succeed in the 21st century, knowledge of and sensitivity to the personal culture and cultural diversity of other organizations and individuals is essential. We're not just referring to obvious cultural elements based on ethnic origins, age, gender, religion, national identity, geography, food, clothing, and the popular culture. We're also talking about the values and nuances of behavior that combine in "how these guys do business". Many times, just acknowledging the cultural interests of a partner, prospect or colleague can create a very different level of chemistry, making the business relationship much deeper and more meaningful. Transorganizations are aware of this and make it a point to be highly sensitive to the diversity of cultures that exist within them and within the other organizations they interact with.

- **Curiosity.** For the individual, there may be no more useful human quality than a lively sense of curiosity. It opens the door to a thousand different worlds of intellectual and experiential exploration and vastly enriches life. This is no less true for the organization.

Transorganizations build a sense of curiosity into their processes. They use it to analyze themselves, their attitudes, their motivations and their goals. They also use it to explore the nature and the needs of their suppliers, their distributors and especially their customers. Finally, they use it to probe the world at large, to reveal any misconceptions they may have, and to uncover the reality of the environment they occupy. Practically, they go to conferences, appear in community events, sports events, NGO boards—and develop a sense of reality.

- **Communities**. In the new world of the 21st century, the ability to see any large group of people as a "community of interest" is a key to marketing success. It's no longer possible for organizations to create a "wide profile" of consumers and customers—there's too much diversity among them and the mix is constantly changing. Instead, organizations should understand that all customers are members of various communities or networks of interest, identity or other common parameters. That understanding will provide unexpected ways to reach and influence customers and to market products and solutions, especially by listening to social networks to understand new social dimensions, new social dynamics, new needs.

Transorganizations are adopting a network and a community-based approach to interacting with customers, because it is in these communities that the conversations relevant to their business are taking place. When possible, they are becoming *members* of the relevant communities, so that they are able to understand the issues, the concerns and the business opportunities they present.

- **"Cuality"**. No, that's not a typo. It refers to a different way of measuring *cus*tomer satisfaction and product q*uality,* the transorganizational way. Traditional corporations typically measured product quality at the factory gate, as viewed and measured by the company's own quality department. Transorganizations go beyond that. They believe that the customer's judgment of the quality of the product offering trumps any internal measurements.

Transorganizations also believe that customers do not judge product quality merely on the product or service. They also factor in style, attitude, the ease of doing business, empathy and similar elements—in other words everything the provider and his service or product offer, throughout its life cycle.

It takes a lot more effort to measure "Cuality" than it does to measure quality against well-defined parameters. But transorganizations know that without a holistic, integrated view of customer experience, they could easily make major business mistakes, lose the loyalty of their customers, diminish brand equity and eventually feel the effects at the bottom line.

Many more "c" words are associated with transorganizations—creativity, communication, collaboration, connectivity, competency, consultation, comprehensive solution offering, comfort-zone marketing, contact enrichment, customer expectations, competitiveness and clarity. These terms, which overlap and reinforce each other, are the transorganization's customary language, and the concepts they represent shape its mindset and drive its behavior.

A Challenge to Transorganizational Efficiency

Every employee or manager in a transorganization is dealing with a dis-ease, one of the by-products of technology. Unlike previous generations, they are unable to plan their time because their day is driven by an ever-increasing number of messages they must process.

We call it "the messorganization dis-ease". The chief symptoms of this dis-ease are stress and inefficiency. No matter how hard someone works, no matter how many hours they put in every day, no matter how intensely they focus or try to focus on the tasks at hand the message trumps everything else, or seems to. The message could be an email, an IM, a fax, a telephone call on a landline or wireless—any digital piece of information that requires attention and response. And it can come from a customer, a business partner, a colleague, an information system or a digital content system. Transorganizations, and those who work for them, have adopted these technologies for the best of reasons—to increase connectedness and efficiency. But all too often, they have an unanticipated side effect: they kill human productivity.

The new communications technology, while it does enable communication, also offers the possibility of continuous interruption of quality time at work, at home and on the road, as well as the continuous interruption of any time spent thinking or planning.

Many executives have told us that one of their biggest problems is the "email monster" inside their laptops and PDAs. They say that every day they receive so many emails that it is impossible to answer all of them—even though they know that an unanswered message can mean neglecting some important business, or insulting someone who is waiting for answer.

Unfortunately, the new communications technology has a peculiar effect on some people. It transforms them into what we call "email bombardiers", who flood the system with lengthy responses to every email they receive and send their replies to many more people, "just FYI". And some people add to this, by sending you one email, then sending another email to see if you've received the first one, then a thank-you email responding to your reassurance, then an email of complaint, saying that your answer didn't come soon enough.

When you multiply that by 100 or 200 or more—on a daily basis—what might be a simple annoyance becomes practically disabling. Response-hungry email behavior creates high levels of stress to those who have much more to do than simply answer their emails. It shifts them from planning to responding. And when individuals and teams need to respond to an increasing number of emails, there is less time to think, create, innovate and reflect.

Is there a cure for "the messorganization disease"? We think there is, in the emergence of a new generation that has almost genetically transformed itself to deal with digital communications tools. We're talking about people who were born in 1985 or later. These young people have learned to process short messages very effectively. They do not read—or write—long documents. They are exceedingly comfortable in a multi-processing multi-media environment and very skilled at switching focus from one medium to another. They are used to SMS, chatrooms and forums, they use the "textspeak" version of English. They understand symbols. They can access, evaluate and purge information very quickly. They have the skill to decide which messages are important.

Unfortunately, this generation is just entering the workforce, and usually in junior positions. Afflicted "messorganizations" are learning skills from this generation in order to better manage this dis-ease. They need to develop ways to respond faster and faster, to quickly identify the essence of written materials, to master the language of brevity and to learn how to resist the temptation of reading or writing useless emails.

Is Your Organization Ready to be a Transorganization?

These are the key characteristics of transorganizations.

Here are some questions to consider, based on feedback from executives newly introduced to transorganizational concepts.

- What do you really know about your customers' experience with your organization? How about not just your external customers, but everybody in your company you serve and whose expectations you need to exceed? If you think you don't know enough, how do you plan to find out?

- Do the people in your organization easily cooperate and create coalitions when you're facing crises or challenges that require multidisciplinary approaches? Or are the boundaries between departments and functions strong and impenetrable?

- Does your organization maintain skills and competencies that are seldom or no longer needed?

- Do you know, right now, which parts of your organization and which key people are generating plenty of energy and which are struggling?

- Are you (and your organization) sometimes the victim of your perfectionism and need for complete control or flawless performance? If so, can you dial down your intensity and accept the idea that "good enough" is sometimes exactly that, so that you can focus on matters that really need to be handled flawlessly.

- Does your organization have a soul—with the six dimensions we described and a clear and well-developed set of values, motivations and visions for the future? Does it have clarity on its core business? Is it aware of its stakeholders' collective experience? Does it have financial awareness, information sensors, and knowledge management practices? Does it have an aligned brand identity? And does it act in accordance with this identity, in all of its interactions with customers, suppliers, distributors, and internal personnel?

- Do you think of your team members not just as occupying slots on the company organization chart, but also as people with rich and important second lives?

- Does your organization have a complex, specialized, multi-level hierarchy, in which there is great distance from top to bottom and strong walls between departments?

- Does your organization generally measure productivity and performance on the basis of results and impact, or on the basis of effort and results?

- Are you the leader of a messorganization, in which many key employees are so overwhelmed by the volume of email and other electronic communications that they do not have the time to think, organize, plan and handle their jobs in a rational manner?

- Is your organization positioned to quickly and efficiently find, contract and engage external competence with outside partners? And has your organization created a shared set of goals with its outside partners?

- Does your organization think of its products or services as its natural output, which customers should learn to accept, or does it see its products and services as experiences, to be evaluated and reshaped, as necessary, by customer needs and opinions?

Part Four: Characteristics of the Transleader

Experience has shown that looking into the future is most useful when it is at the beginning, not the end, of a significant conversation.
Peter Schwartz[1]

Leaders of organizations need vision and courage to shape, inspire and drive them forward. However, people who think and act in many different ways from conventional CEOs lead transorganizations. The way of Henry Ford, Thomas Watson and Jack Welch—the way of the heroic CEO, the great man at the top—has lost traction. It's been made obsolete by a new era, which demands a new kind of leadership.

Transleadership is the name we have given to this new dynamic role, and the true transleader is riding on a wave of change.

What makes the transleaders different from their predecessors? It's not so much that they employ different techniques. In fact, traditional CEOs often practice some fragments of transleadership, but they do so haphazardly, without understanding the larger picture of transleadership.

The heart of the difference is that transleaders have *chosen* their path. They have taken responsibility for themselves at the very deepest level, and their leadership style, words and deeds, are *intentional,* the product of self-awareness and introspection.

Transleaders have made a promise to themselves and are keeping it: not to fool themselves about anything, to recognise the lens through which they view themselves, their people, their organizations, their circumstances and their world, because they know that they cannot broaden their "reality" if they deny it.

Transleadership is presented here as an ideal model of behavior, skills and attitude, against which individuals can benchmark themselves.

What are the major characteristics of Transleaders? We claim they are the following:

---

1   Schwartz, Peter. *The Art of the Long View* Currency Doubleday, 1991.

1. They see themselves through a prism—their soul, and have the ability to see the world around them through varying lenses.
2. They exercise power by sharing leadership.
3. They make an impact at a distance.
4. They are the masters of Agility.
5. They are restlessly innovating.
6. They look at the world from a distance, defying gravity.
7. They welcome diversity.
8. They master the balance between focus and flexibility.

Let's look at each of these characteristics.

1. How the Transleader Sees Himself and the World

Transleaders see themselves and look at their organizations and the world in which it operates from a distance, seeking perspective and breadth of view. They refuse to act like Plato's man in a cave, hoping to discern reality by studying the shadows on the cave's walls. They don't limit themselves to the inside view. They are ready to go beyond their immediate environment to acquire a greater perspective. Transleaders need to be able to develop perspectives of their business and markets through different lenses, with a much broader scope; like Astronauts see the planet Earth from outer space, they should be able to defy the traditional views, by being less attached to the perspectives, opinions, analyses and studies of their "market space", and be able to see beyond the traditional observation posts, from a distance. In a way, the challenge of the Transleaders is to be able to develop the perspectives of astronauts while keeping both feet on the ground.

We typically find leaders who look at the world from a very narrow perspective—their company, their market, their industry—and do not pay attention to the bigger picture that is the full scope of events or deep trends that are shaping and re-shaping their business. Most of them think that these changes are not always "relevant to their business". That's where transleaders are very different—they develop a whole different range of sensors through which they acquire more information and intelligence about what's really relevant—even if it does not look like this at first sight.

What do they look for? Whatever isn't obvious—unexpected insights, unlikely serendipities, and subtle variations in the marketplace, both tangible and intangible. They look for small things that weren't there the last time they looked, or the sudden absence of something they expected to see. They scour the landscape for changes of any kind or size.

They also listen, proactively. They are in constant dialog with their markets, their distributors, their sales forces, their customers, their production teams and everyone else whose views, experiences or perspectives might extend their vision.

Transleaders recognize that they are not all-knowing. They recognize that their employees and their customers are dynamic and multifaceted, and that they too are motivated by hopes and dreams and challenges, and by their efforts to come to terms with an ever-changing world.

Transleaders will look at themselves, both from the inside and from the outside, the better to know who they really are. They assess, measure, analyze and observe themselves dispassionately and truthfully, resisting any urges they may have to tell themselves what they want to hear rather than what they need to hear. They try to determine the boundaries, the character and the constituent elements of their "soul".

The Transleader's Prism of their Soul

Let's define what we mean by the "soul" here. Transleaders look at themselves through a six-dimensional prism. This can be seen in the diagram above. We think that the soul of transleaders goes beyond the "spiritual" aspects—it combines spiritual, emotional and material aspects together. And we believe that the level of self-awareness and, more importantly, the sense of responsibility to these dimensions, are the key building blocks of the transleader's "soul".

Fully evolved and self-aware transleaders will require energy, optimism and creativity. They will face many complex and fast-paced challenges and will need these qualities to take advantage of problems, and to find a way to overcome them.

Transleaders are not only creative, but are also intuitive. They make connections that other people don't make and can draw accurate conclusions from apparently insufficient information. They know this about themselves, and because of this they are intrinsically confident: confident enough to take risks, confident enough to fail and yet to end up stronger.

Transleaders are not lone wolves. They enjoy and find satisfaction in sharing. As a result, they are inviting, not standoffish. They are comfortable with diversity and, at their core, are fundamentally inclusive and respectful, both to people and ideas. They have a great deal of empathy for both.

Others experience them as they really are. They are easy to know, because they will be transparent and open about themselves and their feelings. They are neither deceptive nor manipulative, but are inherently honest. They are authentic and genuine.

Finally, transleaders are in harmony with themselves. Their words and actions are consonant with their inner being. Their work and personal relationships are not burdened with hidden conflicts and hidden agendas. They are not seething with unresolved inner conflicts.

As a result, transleaders are clear and focused. They know who they are and they know what their role is, and that knowledge informs their every word and deed. They not only know their soul, they honor it.

2. How the Transleader Exercises Power by Sharing Leadership

By temperament or by choice, transleaders are neither control freaks nor perfectionists. They are well aware of their human limitations and they know they have a finite amount of time and energy, and that they must use their resources wisely.

Transleaders do not see themselves as monarchs of the corporation. They do not seek to dictate policy or decisions. Instead, their goal is to share the decision-making with their team, and not only the decision-making, but also the responsibility for it—even the leadership role. This is the CEO as orchestra conductor. All of the sections of the orchestra have their leaders—the strings, the woodwinds, the brass—but the conductor is the leader of the leaders. So is the transleader.

Transleaders others into the process and give them each an important and sometimes a decisive voice. They rarely give orders, working instead for wholehearted agreement, and relying on the resulting trust. They are more like mentors than bosses. And as mentors, they are more inclined to empower others than to claim omniscience. They only get as involved as they need to be, not as some protocol requires. They give up the power of command in return for the power of influence, trust and respect.

Leadership-sharing has several advantages. First, it's the equivalent of putting more wheels on the bus, giving it greater stability in the event of a flat tire. Second, it's real-life, real-time training for the next generation of leaders. Third, it ensures that major decisions benefit from a variety of perspectives, reducing unexpected risks and expanding the company's ability to spot new opportunities.

Sharing leadership means sharing risks as well as opportunities, and it also means sharing the mistakes and the failures. And there will be some of each. How do transleaders react to mistakes and failures—their own, and those of their team members? They accept them, learn what they can from them, and move on as quickly as they can.

What they don't do is waste time with useless ruminating. They don't let mistakes or failures—theirs or others—stop them from taking more risks. Most importantly, they analyze instead of placing blame. They don't judge those who've made mistakes or failed, rather they help them learn from what happened. They elevate their people and show appreciation, if only for their willingness to take risks.

Benjamin Zander, conductor of the Boston Philharmonic Orchestra, conducts classes at a prestigious music school. When his students arrive on the first day, he tells them that he knows they are worried about what grade they'll get in his class.

"Don't worry", he says "I'm going to give you all an 'A'—on one condition. The condition is this: Before I give the grade, you must submit a letter to me describing how accomplished a musician you expect to be when you finish my class."

Then, for the rest of the course, he holds them to their word, helping them achieve what they hoped to achieve—encouraging and praising them all the way, taking note of even the slightest accomplishment. "And they earn their 'A's", he has said. "By the end of the year, they *are* what they hoped to be, almost without exception."

Transleaders have a similar attitude toward the people with whom they work. They want to boost self-confidence and help build knowledge and skills. They are not preoccupied with finding fault and they refuse to belittle. They don't do this simply because they're considerate or want to be seen as nice guys. They do it to strengthen their team and their organization.

Transleaders also have a relaxed outlook toward the working style of their team members. They measure their people by results and impact, not by visible effort, the number of hours worked, their attendance record at meetings, their strict adherence to the company dress code or anything else that doesn't affect how well they do their jobs.

Furthermore, transleaders don't try to impose their ideas of comfort and convenience on the rest of their team. They leave these decisions up to the people who are affected by them. They give them space to be, room to grow. This, too, is natural to them.

Numerous studies have shown that when people can't control their environment, their levels of stress and depression increase—and their self-confidence fades. Transleaders know this instinctively. They happily cede all the control they can to their people, which contributes to the health of the organization and its employees, builds self-confidence and personal dignity, and is tangible evidence of the transleader's trust and respect.

3. How the Transleader Makes an Impact at a Distance

In an 800-person organization 10 to 15 years ago about 95% of employees would come into the office and 5% would be out on the road selling. An organization might have consisted of one big building or three offices. Most of the time, executives, team leaders and business managers would be in close physical proximity.

Now, in the same organization, some people work from home, and a greater percentage work on the road. There are many more home offices and branch offices. Headquarters might now be on a single floor in a Manhattan office building and the physical distance between managers and employees has grown dramatically.

This story is typical. The small-and-medium-sized organizations of the 21st century are not set in the company towns of the 19th and 20th century. They're spread out all over the map, often all over the world—branches, factories, research facilities, distribution centers, sales offices. This means it's physically impossible for any CEO, no matter how hard he or she tries, to keep an eye on everything.

Even when it comes to employees at the headquarters office, CEOs may have a hard time overseeing their chief team members, who may be traveling, working at home, visiting a distant branch or otherwise unavailable. Creating presence when the reality is absence is clearly quite a challenge. In these situations, CEOs can no longer deploy face-to-face personal impact, or communicate through their exuberance or charisma.

For a control-freak leader, a CEO who grudgingly allows his people to work at home on special occasions, and even then calls them every half hour, or emails them every 15 minutes or constantly instant-messages them, this is not easy to accept. It's not easy for his employees either. They experience him as being intrusive and untrusting.

Transleaders have developed a skill to help them deal with this situation. It's called "making an impact from a distance". It's based on their awareness that since they cannot always be present at crucial moments, they need to find a way to implant their ideas and values in their people's hearts and minds, so their influence is on-going.

Two major skills are required in order to make an impact from a distance. The first is the ability to trust people. The second major skill is the ability to communicate intent with clarity, simplicity and passion.

One CEO we met had just internalized a new business strategy which represented a quantum leap for the company, requiring a major transformation of the company's business competence, target markets, business models and operations. He internalized the new vision and strategy so deeply that his passion was apparent to everyone with whom he came into contact—whether face-to-face, through telephone calls, by video conference, through emails, etc. The CEO became a walking broadcaster—with passionate communication skills. His belief in the future he had chosen for his organization was so strong and so sincere that he injected the essence/DNA of what he was thinking not only into his team, but into many others in the organization, even winning the loyalty of the company's traditional customers. In this way, he managed to become a "mental presence" in the minds of his sales people. In any meeting, when listening to people talking, he would ask—"how should we rephrase our language if we want to win in the new market we are developing?" The power of reframing the company's jargon, concepts and terms definitely started to pay off; after all, the CEO could not have met every employee face-to-face. Yet new linguistics, new communication styles, and the use of a shared language create a cultural shift and spread through the organization.

By doing this, the CEO demonstrated one of the best ways to make an impact from a distance: to espouse his views with passion and clarity. Yes, the change he was announcing was challenging, but it was also vibrant and exciting, and people tend to align around that kind of change, especially when the existing paradigm is boring and stale.

He also shared his "soul" with his team—not just the transformation, but also the deep, underlying reasons for it. The elements of transleadership cannot be fully communicated to others with logic and facts. People need to sense, hear and deeply appreciate why the transleader believes certain ideas or strategies are so important. So this CEO, like other transleaders, let people hear what drove him, made them privy to his inner beliefs and vision. He distilled and passionately internalized his vision and inspired his team so that it became their thinking as well.

Geographical, conceptual and cultural distance is not difficult for the transorganization. Transleaders use language that can be shared with passionate enthusiasm in every form of communication, and if transleaders communicate their deep personal conviction, not just their "logical analysis", then it becomes an opportunity for a new conversation within the organization, and for transformational thinking.

Just as transleaders are clear about who they are, in their "soul", they are clear about their vision for the company. In general terms, they know what they hope to achieve and have a pretty good idea of how they think it can be achieved. They communicate that vision to everyone in the organization not just once, but repeatedly, adjusting the message as circumstances change.

And communicating the vision is just the beginning. Transleaders actively seek their employees' input and approval. They do not want to *dictate* their vision to the rest of the team, but to infuse it into their genes, so that it is as much the employees' vision as it is theirs.

Finally, transleaders do their best to make sure that their "soul" is in harmony with the "souls" of the organization's other key people. And through recruitment and retention they intentionally build an organization that is intrinsically in tune with their vision.

By consciously using all of these techniques, transleaders make an impact even on those employees whom they may seldom see face-to-face. It is a necessary and effective method of motivating an entire company.

And let's face it, you can't motivate someone through hands-on, in-your-face presence. People aren't comfortable with someone looking over their shoulder all the time. They don't want to be constantly monitored, or frequently interrupted. They want to work within their comfort zones.

Letting them do this is a powerful way to express trust and respect. It is a way of saying, "I measure your value by your impact and the results you bring, not by the time you spend in the office or the way you dress. I am giving you freedom for self-expression, self-development, self-motivation—because I believe that people can elevate. I want to elevate you. I don't want you to waste time commuting to the office, if working from home makes you more comfortable."

What we're saying here applies not only to small-to-medium-sized businesses, but to organizations of all kinds. On one occasion, we were called in by the chief of a major police department and asked to help him figure out how to prevent his forces, which were spread over a wide area, from making serious errors.

"I depend on my officers in remote locations", he told us. "I depend on them—I have no choice—to go to after criminals, to capture them, to bring them in legally. I depend on them to solve problems, to apply departmental values responsibly. And they have to do this in my absence. I can't be there all the time. But if something goes wrong, I'm the one who gets blamed. How do I deal with this?"

We advised that there were two ways. The first was to create multiple layers of command and control. Appoint someone to be your protégé one level below you and have him do the same, all the way down the line. That gives you a strong scheme of enforcement, reporting, monitoring.

But this, we told him, is a bad idea. It's expensive and it's intrusive. It's discouraging to individual development. And your officers will feel that you don't trust them to make the right decisions in your absence. When you do that, you eliminate important sources of energy. It has a negative effect on the entire force.

The entire strength of the police force, we said, depends on people doing the right things when you are not there. So what can you do to make sure you are present at any event without being there? What is it in you, as a professional leader, that you want your people to take with them on every police call? Beyond training, tools and weapons—how can you make them hear your voice in the field?

The chief understood where we were leading him. "I need to better articulate my values and expectations", he finally said. "I need them to know my preferences—when to call and involve me and when to handle things by themselves.

"And that's just the first thing. The second thing is that now I understand that I cannot punish my people for the mistakes they make. My role is to make sure their mistakes are small, and that I can help fix them. I want them to avoid the big mistakes, but I also want them to be not afraid to make decisions."

Making an impact at a distance is not an intuitive skill. It must be learned and consciously practiced. And to become effective at it, transleaders have to give up some comfortable old habits. But when they do, the rewards are significant.

4. The Agility of the Transleader

One of most important assets of a transleader is *agility*. Looking at agility from the outside, it's pretty easy to define. It's the ability to quickly adjust to changing circumstances, to unexpected threats or opportunities, to turn on a dime. But for a transleader, agility is much more complex than that. We see agility as composed of resilience, responsiveness and reflection.

First of all, transleaders are *resilient*—that is, they recuperate quickly. They may be shocked, surprised or even knocked for a loop, but it doesn't take long for them to regain their composure.

Resilience is a quality that begins with self-knowledge. Resilient people know and acknowledge their strengths and weaknesses, and do so without false modesty or embarrassment. They strengthen themselves where they are most vulnerable, and continually sharpen their skills.

At the same time, transleaders are sufficiently self-confident to admit their errors and, when appropriate, to apologize for them. That's part of their dedication to reality and evidence of their willingness to acknowledge responsibility. This attitude allows transleaders to accept their failures, to not let themselves become paralyzed by their mistakes and to move on to the next challenge with confidence and a belief in themselves. And this earns respect from their employees, while providing a model for them.

Another element of transleader agility is *responsiveness*. Transleaders intentionally set themselves to be responsive and reactive in several ways. It is not just about the "speed" of reaction, it is about the appropriateness of the response. They take a continual inventory of their surroundings, their circumstances, their people, the competitive environment, the culture that surrounds them, advances in technology, social trends—everything and anything. Metaphorically, transleaders sit in a mental crow's nest, so that they are the first to see a ship come over the horizon and the first to be able to identify it. To fortify and extend their vision, transleaders continually observe and listen to an organization's employees and, just as importantly, its customers. They maintain an internal communications system in which they are the chief client, sending out questions and requests, and ask for truth and depth in return. They do not use this channel to transmit orders and commands, but to receive unvarnished information.

Transleaders are not only alert to changes of any kind, they prepare for them in advance. They anticipate where they should be, how their organization should be positioned, what to make of the changes that come into their field of vision, and how to act.

Another factor that contributes to transleader agility: their ability and inclination to *reflect* on themselves and their situation. They ask powerful questions of themselves and others—How much time and effort are you willing to put into this project? What personal qualities can you deploy to improve your organization's chances of success? What personal weaknesses do you have that could endanger this success? Have you bought into this effort on an emotional level? What kind of help do you need to be really effective here? What are your reservations? Do you have the energy for this work? Do you see your situation as an opportunity or a problem? What will you do if X happens, or Y or Z?

When transleaders have these answers in hand, they analyze them carefully, taking a continual inventory of their organization's readiness, either to handle what might be anticipated or what cannot be anticipated.

They also keep a close eye on their own and their company's overall health—physical health, emotional health, positive attitude, firing on all cylinders—because agility is most pronounced in companies that are already strong and healthy.

5. How a Transleader Leads Restlessly

Elements of the transleader's style can sometimes be found in the actions of traditional CEOs, as the product of their personalities or characters or their experience. The full panoply, however, is reserved for transleaders who have found this leadership style within themselves or intentionally changed their style to coincide with the principles of transleadership.

Transleaders are never satisfied with "more of the same", even when sales and profits are high and turnover is low. They lead with a clear awareness that continuing to do things the way they've always been done—*even if it's working*—is not a recipe for growth. They also know that when an organization isn't growing, it is in danger of shrinking.

This means that transleaders are intrinsically willing to consider something new, and, if they decide it makes sense, to change course, even if the organization has to give up a path that's tried and true.

While transleaders are intensely interested in the future, especially as it pertains to their organization, they do not base their decisions on simplistic future forecasts and projections. There are two important reasons for this:

First, they know that forecasts and projections say more about the past than they do about the future. They use the past as a baseline and subject that baseline to assumptions, which, in turn, are based on assumptions. And all of these assumptions can be voided in minutes by a single event, such as 9/11 or the world financial crisis following September 2008. While the economic crisis, which is still going on, will be temporary, there is a great need to rethink the basic economic model that the world has relied upon. That's why over-reliance on the past might be a fundamental mistake. A new vision will be required in order to continue to be successful.

Secondly, they aren't terribly interested in going with the flow or latching onto a trend. Their goal is to *make* trends, to create the future, through their words and deeds, through their imagination, through their daring, especially through their vision.

Transleaders view the future forthrightly and with courage. They understand the risks of change, but are not paralyzed by them. They are able to focus on what the future has to offer instead of being fixated on protecting what they already have.

For the transleader, the future offers not just a set of options from which to select, but also an unlimited number of possibilities. And that attitude, as we will see, is the bedrock of transorganizational strategy.

Transleaders are not easily discouraged. They have staying power. Within the organization, they are marathon runners. They understand that organizations sometimes take a long time to accept and digest major changes. After all, there are several layers of management to penetrate, even in relatively flat organizations, even in organizations built for change.

6. The View from a Distance

True transleaders are, we believe, high-fliers in the sense that they are always looking down from above—far above—so they can not only see every part of their organization, but also the lay of the landscape around it. They have a much broader perspective on the marketplace, about social and economic trends, about the global realities, than anyone who is standing at sea level.

We're talking about what goes on in transleaders' minds and about the experiences that contribute to their perceptions. We're talking about their unexpected lines of communication within the organization, and beyond it. We're talking about the meetings and conferences they attend where they are the only CEO in the room. We're talking about the books they read and the people they befriend.

All of this gives transleaders a clearer, deeper view of the reality in which the corporation operates, and it gives them strategy-developing tools that conventional CEOs aren't even aware of.

A few years ago, we were consulting with a mid-sized bank lead by a CEO with genuine transleadership qualities. The bank had reached a decision, a good 18-months before its competitors, to "go global". But the bank had limited resources. It couldn't put branches in several new countries and it couldn't blanket every city in whatever country it chose. If it wanted to establish a significant foreign presence, its effort had to be very focused. The transleader listened to his team discuss the possibilities, and occasionally asked questions. They quickly narrowed their choice down to one Asian country, where they had some connections and about which they had some knowledge.

Then they discussed cities. As it happened, they found three major cities in this country, all close enough that an operation in one could support operations in the other two, a good situation for an initial investment that could fairly easily be expanded. The branch would take five years to become fully operational.

"Shouldn't we be aiming at specific customers?", the CEO asked innocently, and the discussion was off again. They finally decided that the customers they were most likely to attract were college and graduate students in the 18-24 year age range, people who might not yet have bank accounts in their own names, but who expected to build professional careers in financial services, high tech and bio-tech. These people could be the core of a loyal customer base that would be active for decades.

The CEO asked another innocent question: "How old are these potential customers right now?" And the rest of his team suddenly realized that they'd been talking about teenagers—Asian teenagers—about whom they knew practically nothing.

This raised a number of questions: What would make us attractive to them? Why would they choose our bank rather than another? What are their ambitions and goals? What difficulties do they have to overcome? How did their families play into their choices? What sort of salaries could young college graduates expect? What was their attitude toward savings, loans, interest rates, etc.?

We returned to the bank's headquarters a year after they had decided on their growth strategy and found that the bank's expansion team had turned into anthropologists. They were studying the profiles, behavior and culture of their potential future customers, and understanding them in depth.

By the time the strategic plan was ready, the bank's team understood not just their potential customers' financial hopes and habits, but their fashions, their music, their career considerations, their approaches to marriage and family, etc. And it was clear that this understanding significantly improved their chances of success.

This organization benefited tremendously from their leader's ability to hover above the landscape and look at the proposed changes with a perspective that was both wide and deep.

What makes a CEO into a transformational leader? The overarching quality is a deep, abiding and unquenchable curiosity, the simple desire to know more—about everything you come in contact with, but especially about people, communities, new ideas, all that is different from what you know.

Leaders who do not have or are unable to cultivate intense curiosity, who prefer to surround themselves with the familiar, the known and the expected, who are not willing to step out of their current mindsets and territories are very unlikely to become transformational leaders. They may make superb managers, but they cannot be counted on to provide a vision for the future.

7. Welcoming Diversity

The transleader's curiosity is a perfect fit with the business environment of the 21st century. We are living in an increasingly multicultural world, a world that will make the 20th century seem positively monochromatic. The 21st century is about racial diversity, ethnic diversity, cultural diversity, philosophical diversity, geographical diversity, gender diversity, age diversity, educational and experiential diversity, and often several kinds of diversity at once.

Transleaders have a natural curiosity that will automatically lead them to ask about and learn about the elements of diversity they come into contact with. Diversity + curiosity = a new synthesis of information, understanding and, quite frequently, unexpected flashes of insight which lead to finding solutions to difficult problems, business problems.

This way of thinking teaches the transleader to think about similar problems in different ways. It is one thing, for example, to ratchet up a business to appeal to Asian teenagers and quite another to appeal to the same age group of Eastern Europeans. Transleadership acknowledges and respects that diversity and builds offerings and solutions that can easily be calibrated to meet specific needs and taste. This applies not only to a company's specific product or service, but to its business model, its distribution system, the ease of doing business, business practices and operational flexibility.

Transleaders are courageous enough to accept and welcome diversity and even impossible combinations in their businesses. And that attitude acts as a greenhouse for the seeds of creativity.

8. Focus vs. Flexibility

What's the easiest way to spot old-style strategic thinking in an organization? We've discovered that when leaders frequently use the word "focus" when they talk about their business, that's a nearly certain sign that he's thinking in traditional P-age terms.

Our observation dates back nearly 20 years, when we were first mastering the basics of business strategy, at a conference held at a UK University. A brilliant lecturer told those of us in his audience that "companies which do not focus on what they are good at... will die"—certainly a striking idea.

He then asked us to look at our own companies and identify our "core business"—and explain why we were spending precious time developing anything else. No one had any good answers.

Ten years later, we reviewed this lesson and discovered, to our surprise, that many companies that had focused with great intensity on their core businesses—a single product line for a single type of customer or a single market—had disappeared or were in trouble. What had happened was simple: their core businesses were no longer valid. The market had changed. And they were so focused that weren't able to change course.

In the mid-1970s, a brilliant group of software engineers at VisiCalc developed the electronic spreadsheet. But before they could capitalize on their invention, a major player emerged and became the market leader—Lotus, of course.

Lotus had had a brilliant insight—that electronic spreadsheets were useful not only to accountants, but to engineers, managers, project managers and many others, so long as the spreadsheet was made compatible for the early 80s emerging new computing device—the personal computer. They'd found—created—a wonderful market.

But that market died when, in the early 90s, Microsoft redefined the scope of professional computer applications, and electronic spreadsheets became just one more element of office automation.

If Lotus had focused deeply on just electronic spreadsheets, it would have been about then that the company found itself in deep trouble. Fortunately, Lotus hadn't obeyed the dictum we heard at that UK University. It was ready with yet another application—Lotus Notes. Lotus founder, Mitch Kapur, had the vision in 1984 to understand that the new phenomena of networked PCs would become the new paradigm in which corporations were to use software applications. That's why in 1984 he formed a partnership with a company called Iris Associates. Lotus started to cooperate with this new innovative group (which was the original developer of notes back in 1973). In 1994, Lotus acquired Iris.

A year later, in 1995, it turned out that Lotus Notes was quite appealing to another major player in the software field, IBM. At the time, IBM wanted to own an automation software suite that would differentiate it from Microsoft. Instead of disappearing, Lotus survived, albeit in another form.

You might ask—what's the difference? They moved from one software application to another one. Yet the difference is in the market, the type of buyer, the business need by the new application—all these redefine the company's "core business"; sometimes, a "small" change in what a company does might look like just another variation on a theme—where in fact it is a much more radical change. And, by the way, companies that want to "diversify" and do not understand that they should be, in fact, expanding and changing their core business—are in great danger of missing the benefits of diversification.

This example demonstrates that even in the P-age, organizations understood that a pure focus on a single product, a single line of business or a single core business was a mistake. Today, transleaders know that there is no real choice between focus and flexibility. Flexibility is the key to survival.

Characteristics of the Transleader: A Summary

Are you a transleader? Is there another transleader in your organization? What qualities can you muster within yourself to become a transleader? To sum them up:

- Transleaders are intelligence officers. They are always looking for the unexpected insight, the unrecognized trends, and the subtle changes in the marketplace. They are information junkies—about the company's markets, customers and technologies. And they maintain a large network of sources and informants.

- They are intuitive and creative people. They deeply understand the business environment and naturally have insights about how to operate within and beyond it.

- They are open and easy to know. They can be trusted and they are able to trust.

- They are marathon runners. They know they recognize changes more quickly than others in their organization and they are well aware of the need to begin, at the earliest opportunity, convincing their colleagues and employees that changes are on the way—that there will be major shifts in business models, competitive landscapes and technology.

- They are encouraging, as opposed to judgmental. They are always inclined to appreciate the efforts and talents of others.

- They reject the "more of the same" option. They recognize that continuity of traditional models is not the road to growth, but the path to stagnation. They are not advocates of the "if it isn't broke, don't fix it" method of operation. If it isn't broke, they are nonetheless eager to figure out how to do it better—before someone else does.

- They are highly flexible, ready to change direction at the drop of a hat if conditions warrant, and are not stuck on pre-determined paths, even if they had personally chosen the old direction.

- They have great clarity, about themselves, about their organization and all of those who have a stake in its products, its services and its success.

- They act like orchestra conductors, drawing great music from their associates, according to the vision they have for the company and in accord with the organization's deepest values.

- They make decisions quickly and surely, gathering the information they need, but not paralyzing themselves with the need to know *everything*.

- They are revolutionary thinkers. They don't spend time trying to figure out how their business can join trends. Instead, they work on ways to generate preference shifts, based on their observations and knowledge of their customers and their markets. They are open to both tangible, rational observations and intangible, immeasurable insights and flashes of inspiration.

- They do not try to forecast the future. Instead, they focus on inventing it. They are fascinated by the possibilities of creating futures of their own design, in which they will control how industries and markets evolve.

- They are both optimistic and stubborn. They know that their openness to change, innovation and in their course alterations will inevitably put them into conflict with members of their teams. They welcome the conflict, because they know it will help them hone their ideas and bring others aboard. They also know that if their ideas are easily adopted, they are not really re-inventing the future, they are simply demonstrating how compliant their employees can be.

- They are excellent listeners. They are highly skilled at eliciting the opinions, observations and preferences of others. As a result, their perspectives are broadened and their information flow is strong and steady.

- They are high energy people. It takes a lot of energy to adopt a broad view of your own organization. It also takes a lot of energy—and determination—to make things happen. Low-energy people seldom, if ever, make good transleaders.
- They understand that their life experiences, their characters and their personalities are at least as important as their professional experiences—in other words, they realize who they are is as important as what they know.
- They are intrinsically curious, eager to know about new people, new trends, new developments, and new ways of doing things.
- They make sure that their leadership is relevant even to those who know more than they do.
- They see themselves less as forceful commanders and more as energetic teachers, social workers, mentors, coaches, guides, conductors and Sherpas.

Transleaders are both born *and* made. For some people, it is a reflection of their natural temperament, personality and character. For others, it is an acquired skill set, taught by life and work experience, by trial and error, learning from their mistakes. For still others, we believe, it is the result of long reflection and self-examination.

In our experience, however, transleaders are—or become—quite conscious of what they are doing and why. They act with an exquisite awareness of their behavioral choices as leaders.

Some food for thought

Most importantly, we suggest that transleaders perform at their best when their souls are aligned with the soul of the transorganization.

The Transleaders and Transorganizations Alignment of Personal and Business Souls

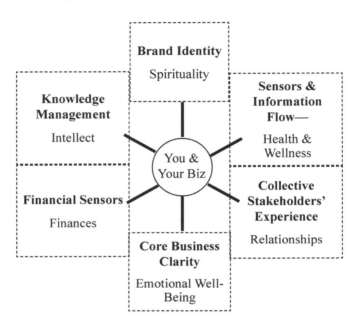

Now you can see how the two prisms should be aligned. We challenge the reader to think what could happen when the transleaders and the transorganizations, through a unified approach, have the same belief and value systems. All we can say is that this is the heart of the leadership challenge—but it is also the key to new levels of success.

Part Five: Transorganizational Strategy

All our knowledge begins with the senses, proceeds then to the understanding, and ends with reason. There is nothing higher than reason.
Immanuel Kant

Over the years, we've worked with many CEOs. But when it comes to a discussion of the importance of business strategy, two CEO types stand out—those who practically reject the idea (regardless of what they say...), and those who accept it but develop flawed attitudes and expectations (believing that strategic planning is a one-time activity which will set a solid strategic plan for the next five years).

In this chapter we would like to talk about attitudes towards strategic thinking, not about "strategies".

One CEO, representing the first type, an engineer by profession, liked to say "When you look backwards and understand what worked, you call it 'strategy'." The other was fond of saying, "The road to the future starts with the next purchase order". (His background was in sales.)

Both dismissed the value of creating a strategic plan and strategic goals. They each felt it was unnecessary and unrealistic make-work, in other words, a waste of time. Reality and conditions change so quickly, and indeed, with our current transorganizational era, market conditions are even more difficult to predict, the shelf life of market is much shorter, so why bother? We did our best to convince them they were wrong. But by the time the engineer-CEO realized it was time to start thinking strategically, it was too late. His company was already unsalvageable. The sales-CEO caught on more quickly. He created a solid strategic plan and put it into operation. In less than two years, he'd changed the DNA of his company and led it to phenomenal growth.

We've seen this result again and again, and yet we've also seen frequent and stubborn resistance to making anything like a strategic plan. The CEOs' resistance to strategic planning does not come from observing the speed of change and telling themselves that making a strategic plan is a futile exercise. From our experience, their resistance to strategic planning is counter-intuitive to their career development as they see it.

They believe that working according to a well-defined strategic plan will limit their ability to show how brilliantly they can innovate and how efficiently they can manage a crisis—both problem-solving skills that make them look like heroes. They also think that writing a strategic plan is risky, because it can turn out to be wrong and make them look foolish. Indeed, making a commitment to a strategic plan requires courage. It is both a huge risk and a huge step for any leader. It also requires—on an ongoing basis—the courage to lead the process of planning scenarios, to define alternatives, to make choices and execute plans, to interrogate your assumptions, to make new decisions—and combine passionate commitment to execute them with deliberate critical thinking about whether the chosen track was the right one. A leader's choice to use a strategy and continuously review and regenerate it is a huge act of courage on his/her part, as it requires intellectual integrity, passion, self criticism and the ability to make mistakes, to admit them and to fix them.

Many leaders have told us, in essence, "Look, I can manage quarterly results and look good. But what's the value of risking making statements about how the marketplace will look 3-4 years from now and exposing myself to criticism if I'm wrong?"

We've heard a lot about "dynamic, opportunity-driven growth based on a portfolio of opportunities" as a viable way of doing business and mitigating risks. That's why large corporations build a portfolio of businesses and try to serve more and more customers in more and more markets. But our experience with many small-to-medium-sized businesses has taught us that they cannot build a portfolio of activities too fast—they have to build critical mass first. Consequently, there is no substitute for strategic planning. The companies that don't do this are almost certain to be caught by surprise.

Of course, strategic planning does not make an organization immune to surprises. On the contrary—if done properly, it prepares the organization to meet the unexpected future, through careful scenario planning. But it does serve as a baseline and a reference point that helps companies understand the magnitude and impact of the unexpected. This is particularly true in the case of companies that—without a strategic plan or vision—opportunistically acquire other businesses. Such companies risk making missteps that could compromise their futures.

Some of the executives who object to strategic planning may do so because they don't really understand it. They may think it's based on some vague, amorphous and intangible idea called "the future". Nothing could be farther from the truth. It's actually based on *results* that can be achieved if you *shape the future* of your transorganization.

Why are these leaders so afraid or unsure of strategy? One of the main reasons, we think, is that they believe it will force them to do something that's much harder than just managing the organization: to think out loud and clearly about what's ahead—what they know, what they don't know and what they want to create.

On the other end of the spectrum, we find CEOs who embrace the idea of developing business strategies, but with the wrong expectations. They look for a solid structure of thinking for a long-term period of five years, which will form the basis for the organization, and they believe that the only way to do it is to focus on the "holy grail" business opportunity that will be the one answer to all challenges ahead. They believe that only through focusing on one significant growth initiative will they be able to maximize the true potential of their business.

Well, this is a risky approach, sometimes worse than ignoring strategy altogether. The expectation that a talented group of people can close its eyes at a given moment in time and decide on its future, without leaving room for agile flexibility down the road, is flawed for two reasons: first, it is somewhat presumptuous, and lacks intellectual integrity and humbleness; and, secondly, the pace of change and the dynamics of markets and business opportunities have dramatically changed over the past 20 years with the windows of opportunity becoming shorter and shorter.

"More of the same—but better" isn't really a business strategy. It's present-oriented, not future-oriented. It's an admirable goal, but it's not the transleader's job. It's a job for professional managers who have hands-on responsibility and who can take current business models and improve performance. This skill set can be applied to almost any operational activity: from improving product stability and quality, to upgrading manufacturing and outsourcing, to more effective marketing, improved customer interaction and collection and cash management.

Transleaders would like all of these areas improved because doing so provides the company with a safety net to build on and because professional line management will be needed to improve the operational excellence required for periods of growth. But improved operational excellence is not, by itself, transformational change or a business strategy for the future. In fact, companies that fall in love with making improvements may blind themselves to the possibilities of transformational change, and damage their chances for survival.

Furthermore, the question isn't how do we get better or make this better. The question is how do we ensure that this product, that process, and those expenses are *relevant*. Relevance changes are based on the macro-picture, the customer and the levels of awareness and insight in the company. Relevance is critical. Better is irrelevant.

For transleaders, what is required is a new balanced approach towards strategic thinking; one that looks at strategic planning with both humbleness and daring determination, one that executes strategies passionately, yet combining self criticism, reflection and constant re-thinking of what's relevant. We call it **Agile Strategic Planning**.

True transleaders focus not just on today's business, but tomorrow's business—tomorrow's results. They are always driving forward, energized not just by what was achieved, but also by what *else* could be achieved. Needless to say, they must look at what was not achieved, but not allow failures to paralyze their thinking.

These transleaders understand the importance of strategic planning. And they continually translate their hopes into a concrete vision and then into an organizational mission. They break this mission into strategic goals and into strategies that can meet these specific goals and results.

This all seems logical enough, but some leaders are unwilling to follow these steps. We often begin a business consultation by asking the company's leaders two simple questions: 1) Do they have a vision and a strategy for their business? And, 2) Can they explain it in language that everyone can understand? Very few can answer these questions with a sufficient degree of clarity or specificity.

If we ask the leaders what they're doing now and what their next step is, this is a question they can answer. But it's the next one that trips them up: How is that next step related to where the organization is going? Usually, this brings the admission that while the next step is very important, it isn't directly related to where they want to go and what they need to do to get there.

The transorganization's Agile Strategic Planning addresses these very questions. It acts like a code of behavior, which, if adhered to, pushes organizations and their leaders to do almost everything a little bit differently. And properly designing it requires genuine soul-searching.

Agile Strategic Planning requires a person to use personal strategic planning at the micro-level so that macro-planning can exist. Let's see how.

Transforming the Organization's DNA

It is our strong belief that transorganizations must use the process of Agile Strategic Planning in order to adopt a strategy of *continual transformation*. But *transformation* requires an explanation. We are not using it as a synonym for "change". When a caterpillar gets larger, that is change not transformation. When it turns into a butterfly, it is transformation. And transformation is irreversible.

For an organization, transformation is nothing less than continually developing your DNA. The result is that it truly becomes something other than it was. You might be asking yourself, about now, "Why would an organization want to alter its identity, at the deepest possible level?"

The reasons are pretty simple: to survive and to grow dramatically.

What we are saying is this: If you want your organization to survive over the long term, you have to adopt a strategy of transformation, continual transformation, moving from peak to peak, with the understanding that nothing is sacred—not tradition, not even the path to the last success.

DNA changes, as you might imagine, are not a small deal. They affect the organization's primary mission, beliefs and values. They are soul-altering. And for that reason, each transformation requires a deep re-harmonization of the company, inside and out, from top to bottom.

As mentioned earlier in the book, many of the employees who were with a company before the transformation might not be the right people to contribute to the altered company. And it isn't a matter of skill. It is because they may have internalized the traditions, habits and limitations from previous years. So transformation requires re-harmonization, a restatement of goals, a re-sharing of beliefs and values, a re-alignment of strategy, leadership and soul. It also requires an in-depth understanding of how people react and accept transformation.

And all transformations, in one way or another, begin with a death—perhaps the death of a product line or the withdrawal from a market, or the death or withdrawal of a leader, and it can be a wrenching and paralyzing experience.

The Principles of Agile Strategic Planning

Transleaders have a very different way of looking at strategy from traditional CEOs. Their strategy is one of transformative change—the outcome of curiosity and adaptability. We found that in many cases the following principles characterize their behavior—and we recommend you follow them:

1. Focus on the future—of the marketplace, of the organization, of the team and of society. Do not dwell on past mistakes or even successes, except to learn from them. When you look at the future, try to identify potential *relevant* scenarios for your market, your customers and your

industry. Do not create a single futuristic vision; instead create a set of potential scenarios—those you believe in, those you hope for, and those you hope will never happen.

2. Aim High—Base the company's business strategy on an overarching and well-defined goal: continuing organizational growth and success. Yet make it ambitious and inspiring. There is a famous saying attributed to Michelangelo—"The greater danger for most of us lies not in setting our aim too high and falling short, but in setting our aim too low, and achieving our mark." It is not a mistake to aim high; the mistake is to aim too low. Make this goal clear to everyone in the organization and make sure everyone is aboard. We have found that once transleaders are committed to a long-term result, such as future revenue figures, they label the strategic plan and brand it with that number. So if you lead company "ABC Inc." with $75m in annual revenues, and your 3-5 year plan is to reach $250m, then "ABC-250" is a simple yet powerful way to charge the imagination and amass the energy of your people.

3. Make a basic strategic decision about the organization—that it will be a predator, not prey. Unlike the past, where acquisitions were the luxury of large companies who reached solid critical mass by growing organically, transorganizations cannot just wait to grow, they need to accelerate growth in parallel—both organically and through mergers and acquisitions. From a much earlier stage compared to the past, they must be ready to make acquisitions and properly integrate acquired businesses.

4. Acknowledge that success is a journey, not a destination. See it as an unending series of milestones, to be reached and exceeded again and again. Think of it not as a mountain to be climbed, but an entire range of mountains, extending toward the horizon as far as the eye can see. And be aware that proclaiming success is the beginning of organizational death.

5. Don't fall into the trap of trying to replicate past successes. Understand that the circumstances that made possible a previous success will never occur again, at least not exactly. New competitors may have entered the market,

consumer needs and desires may have matured, economic conditions may be different, the same personnel may not be available. The whole world may have changed, slightly or significantly, and the differences may be crucial. Trying to replicate past success—and the decision-making style of previous leaders—can be the death of companies, because it omits a central aspect of transleadership: harmonizing the strategy with the soul of the (current) leader.

6. After shaping your future and figuring out where the company is going next, figure out where it's going after that. Habitually look ahead, like a mountaineer checking the trail far in front of him, knowing that his vision will include everything between where he is now and where he wants to go. This means that strategic planning for transorganizations requires the identification of the next achievement, which normally take 1-2 years to ignite, and the following one, which will take 3-4 years to ignite. That journey needs to be at least sketched and spelled out, because as a transleader you need to be prepared for various scenarios. Train yourself to be happy when reaching a peak, to enjoy the moment of fulfillment and achievement, but immediately start moving towards the next one. And by the way, make sure that while you are climbing to one mountaintop, you have already identified the next peak. This is how Agile Strategic Planning happens—whilst you are executing the previous plan, start defining the next one. Begin transformative change when the organization is on its way to the next peak of its success, when resources and morale are at their maximum. Don't wait till you get to the peak... it might be too late to start. Delays just dissipate energy and bring closer the time when change is forced on the company.

7. Actively seek new opportunities for dramatic growth, and resist waiting for an opportunity to present itself. These opportunities may include buying companies ripe for acquisition, entering an under-served market, exploiting a totally new market or a technology that no one has yet capitalized on or even creating a totally new industry if the circumstances are right.

8. Harmonize the company's vision with the expectations of its customers, employees, its distributors, even its suppliers. The easy, if superficial, way to understand this is to imagine everyone being on the same page. But it's much deeper than that. It means having essentially identical goals, motive and visions. It means having the same understanding of the current situation and opportunities for the future.

9. The opposite of harmony is conflict—and nothing is more debilitating to an organization than conflict in the ranks. It saps energy and creates weaknesses. In an orchestra, conflict leads to dissonance, which the conductor must locate and eliminate. He or she must make sure that everyone is playing his or her proper role, and that each individual is personally involved in making his vision—your vision, the company's vision—a reality.

10. Less than 30% of acquisitions fulfill their initial promise. Why? Because the acquisition analysis didn't look at human group dynamics or the energy level of the acquired firm's managers. Most importantly, it didn't examine the other company's soul. It made no effort, or an inadequate effort, to make sure the two companies would harmonize. It probably didn't understand itself well enough either.

11. Accept the possibility of failure, and if it occurs, learn from it—and move on as quickly as possible. Transorganizations don't have time to ruminate, and punishing the guilty party is very often counter-productive. Instead, transorganizations must look forward and find new opportunities.

The leader of a successful corporation can choose between a number of alternative strategies, but only a few are truly transformational. Only a few can maximize the potential of an organization.

Detecting Transformational Opportunities

Transleaders have a knack of detecting transformational opportunities. They use two major techniques:

Customer discovery. Using this technique, the transleader conducts thorough studies of one or more top customers, the object being to learn everything possible about the customers and the environment in which their business operates. Then the transleader invites these customers to a comfortable off-site location for a day-long meeting, telling them that he and his people are engaged in an internal debate about where they want to take their company.

The transleader begins the conversation by throwing out a few tentative ideas and soliciting his customers' opinions. He steers the conversation toward his customer's plans and intentions for themselves, personally, and for the organizations they work for.

The result is a deep exchange of views, ideas and strategies, an intimate dialog of joint discovery, in which the transleader learns what his customers are thinking, where they want to go, and how they see their own business strategy.

Then the transleader asks his customers what products or services might help them reach their goals—not how his company can help, but what they might need, what they could put to good use.

Almost without exception these conversations, if conducted honestly and openly with the genuine intent of helping and providing services, turn out to be eye-openers. They provide a wide range of ideas and possibilities for providing "more to the same."

Shift-sensing. In our years of business experience and consultation with the SMB sector, we have observed that society experiences cycles of change. When—or even whether or not—these changes can be successfully introduced to the marketplace depends on the interplay of two forces: 1) the emergence of technological change and mega-trends and 2) the decline of blocking forces, both inside organizations and within society. These blocking forces are all various forms of resistance to change.

We've analyzed this interplay and have made some interesting discoveries. Mega-trends take about 30 quarters—7-8 years—to reach the point of no return. That is, to become an acceptable concept. (For example, the move to IP telephony was first mentioned in 1996, but only began to materialize in 2003.)

Major innovation trends also take about 30 months to reach the point of no return. Once organizations acknowledge the initial concepts and begin prototyping, it takes about 30 months to produce a stable, sellable product or solution.

Organizational resistance to new technology also revolves around the number 30—but weeks, not months. That's the length of a typical sales cycle for an innovative shift.

At the same time, each technology and customer-base pair are undergoing capability shifts (on the technology side) and needs shifts (on the customer side). Using the 30-30-30 formula, it is usually possible to figure out when needs and technology shifts are aligned.

These are some of the tools that transleaders use to create future growth areas.

The Value of Transformation

When creating their organization's business strategy, transleaders seek out the visions for the future that are truly transformative, because they strongly believe that transformational business strategies offer their organization the greatest chance for dramatic growth and long-term survival.

Transformative change is almost always major surgery. It often means not only taking on enormous new challenges, but also discontinuing operations once considered integral to the company's identity and initial success.

Transformative change is inevitable. It is also necessary, no matter how well a company might be doing. This is a lesson many championship sports teams have learned. They realize that they must change—improve, that is—if they expect to win again. Why? Because their stars will be older, because their opponents will be better, because the combination of circumstances that made them champions may not occur again.

Once upon a time, shareholder value was created almost entirely by operational excellence and hard work. But times have changed. Capital markets no longer focus, laser-like, on operational excellence. In fact, they have come to realize that it's risky for a company to focus on operational excellence at the expense of transformational growth.

Today, capital markets want to hear why a company will be successful over time. They want to know why their capacity, their technology, their marketing position, their human capital and their cash make them more prepared for growth than their competitors.

This is why companies sometimes publish great quarterly results only to see their shares drop. The markets were expecting something else that was not delivered: passion, promise, vision, and excitement. They want to see a determination to be more, with a quest for greatness.

Whether or not they do that depends on the vision and courage of the transleader. It depends on his ability to realize that he can choose his future and the future of his company. The possibilities truly are his to create.

A visual representation of the shift toward Agile Strategic Planning:

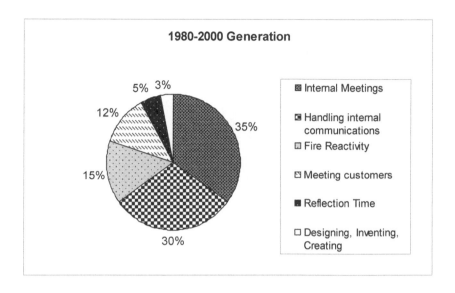

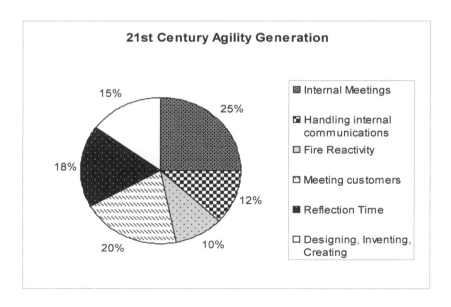

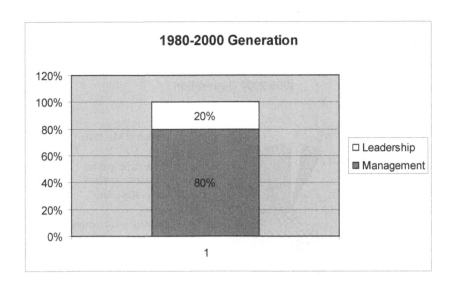

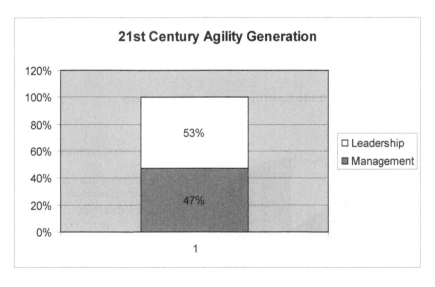

Part Six: Practices of Intentional Transleadership

Tell me and I'll forget; show me and I may remember; involve me and I'll understand.
Chinese Proverb

What is a transleader? Most likely, he or she is currently—or prospectively—the CEO of a small-to-medium-sized business or the head of an organization of similar size, the person who has the primary responsibility for its survival, its success and its growth. But the transleader is a new kind of CEO.

The transleader is someone who looks at himself, his company and his people in a new way, a way that is consonant with society and the marketplace as it is today, not as it was when he got his MBA, or his first office on the executive floor.

Compared to the previous generation of CEOs, transleaders are more agile in that they are more resilient, responsive, and reflective. Their resilience is their ability to leverage failures and breakdowns in the company and create learning experiences for all. Their responsiveness is demonstrated by their ability to hold multiple realities together as they flex their style and mental models to the needs and concerns of their particular audience, and are much more likely to consider customers' and employees' insights as valuable as their shareholders'. Transleaders design in "quiet reflective" time for themselves and their teams to get out of the "noise" and the "action" so they can gain perspective. These leaders keep vigilant records of what they expect to happen and what actually occurs. Every opportunity to practice and strengthen their agility is taken.

They are also more likely to find themselves running stronger, more vibrant, faster growing, more impactful and more successful companies, companies better positioned to survive and thrive in a highly competitive and rapidly changing market. They are any company's best bet for the future. And those who behave as transleaders are more likely not only to succeed, but to live full and satisfying lives.

What does it take to be a transleader? A minority of corporate executives have it in their DNA. The vast majority must find it within themselves, by becoming more conscious of who they are, how they behave, how they relate to those within the organization and those on the outside who have an impact on it. They must make a purposeful decision to embrace the elements of transleadership. In our experience, most people do not experience this as changing themselves, but as awakening, as understanding, as "getting it" like never before.

The foundation of transleadership begins with a determined, clear-eyed and continuous search for the most pertinent view of reality.

Searching for Reality

As the CEO of a small-to-medium-size business, or a similar organization, you are by necessity a creature of information. You immerse yourself in it, hoping to understand the business environment, hoping to get a clear picture of how your organization is doing, hoping to spot opportunities and avoid dangerous surprises.

Yet no matter how smart you are, how hard you work, how much information you process, you are well aware that you could be blind-sided by something you did not anticipate, something you weren't alerted to by that great river of research that crosses your desk every day.

Why is this? In large measure, it's because in the business schools of the 20th century—and on your way up the corporate ladder—you were trained to focus on and evaluate one kind of information, the kind that reaches you in reports, studies, surveys, white papers, charts, Power Point presentations, SEC filings, news stories and the similar information generated by production, marketing and due diligence. You are prepared on what you should know. But you weren't prepared to accept the corner of the Johari window that says, "you don't know what you don't know". Being comfortable with realizing that you have aspects of yourself and your business to which you cannot get access creates humility in your leadership that allows you to conduct a more thorough inquiry.

Johari Window

	known to self	unknown to self
known to others	My Public Self	My Blind Spots
unknown to others	My Hidden Self	My Unconscious Self

Business schools weren't teaching you about a totally different kind of information—most of them still aren't. If they were even aware of it, the corporate leaders you worked for as your career developed paid little, if any, attention to this kind of information.

But the second kind of information has become more and more critical to survival and success in this new world we call the 21st century. In our experience, those who focus on it have a significant competitive advantage over those who don't.

Unlike the first kind of information, with its massive paper trail, the second kind is mainly intangible. It is highly personal. And it is largely internal. It involves thoughts and feelings, hopes and dreams, personal preferences and personal proclivities—yours, your employees', your suppliers' and especially your customers'.

You cannot "plug and play" a white paper into your business to solve a problem. You have to have discernment and also the ability to trust your own judgment. However, the ability to find wisdom from intangibles is a great progressive skill for the 21st century leader.

Taking an Inventory of Yourself

The second kind of information is not secret. If you look for it, if you make the effort, if you ask the right questions of yourself, if you are purposeful and persistent, if you are honest and open-minded, if you make it your intention to find it, it's there for the taking. And making intelligent use of this information will show up in your bottom line.

In this case, as in so many others, wisdom begins with an acknowledgement of your limitations. It begins with the assumption that, despite your most diligent efforts, your picture of reality is incomplete and probably inaccurate in part. To complete it you need the help of others. Even more importantly, you need to look deeply at yourself, for without self-knowledge, an enormous part of the equation is missing.

Who is that man or woman in the corner office, sitting behind your desk? Remember, the success or failure of your organization depends on him—not just his knowledge, intelligence and skill, but on what kind of a person he is: on his personality and character, on his courage and imagination, on his insight and his self-esteem.

How do you find out about that man or woman? You ask questions and you demand complete and honest answers—it's just a conversation with yourself, after all. If you lie, you're the only victim. We're not talking about psychoanalysis here. We're talking about close observation and transparency. The greatest way to gain access to "truth" and to interrogate reality is to be transparent and be a model through your own experience. Stating where you made a mistake or where you made an assumption gives others permission to "admit" areas for continuous improvement or where there was an error. Accountability is driven by choices at the top. That is the DNA that will replicate. If you want more of something inside your organization, you have to model that first. As Russell Ackoff's states as one of his Management F-Laws: "Managers cannot learn from doing things right, only from doing things wrong."

Given the complexity of human beings, the list of potential questions you can ask yourself is endless, but here's a simple suggestion: Which of these words apply to you? Courageous, non-confrontational, cautious, adventurous, pessimistic, even-tempered, patient, suspicious, forgiving, friendly, erratic, loyal, gambler, control freak, fearful, open, biased, imaginative, stubborn, intense—there are many others, but these should make a good start.

You might also ask yourself what drives you, what motivates you, what gets your juices flowing. Is it ambition? Fear? A quest for fulfillment? Pride? Ego? The expectations of others? Criticism? Self-protection? You might ask yourself what makes you feel like you have made the best contribution? Service to others? Leadership? Inspiration? Contribution? Whether your core purpose comes from a place of want or a place of contribution or a combination of these factors, it impacts the way you lead and also the way your organization operates.

What does this have to do with your leadership skills and the chances your organization will survive and thrive? A great deal. Taken together, these qualities are a set of filters through which you view yourself, your work, your company, your associates, your competitors and those who interact with your organization. When you are aware of your filters, you can correct and fine-tune them, giving you a clearer view of reality.

Insights and perceptions will inevitably emerge from this exercise. And if you make a habit of looking at yourself this way, the insights will deepen, offering explanations of past behaviors and guides for the future. CEOs who keep a journal of these internal conversations can create a powerful tool for developing self-knowledge. Journal entries simply stating what was done or reporting key indicators don't really lead to progressive intelligence. Journal entries that yield wisdom for you and your organization are the answers to these sorts of questions: Where could I have been a more effective leader today? Where could I have had more patience? What clue did I miss from that sales call that could have made me have more impact on that supplier?

What this exercise will give you is a clearer picture of how you react to opportunity, or a challenge, good news or bad, success and failure. It will tell you what you can expect from yourself, and why and in what ways you are likely, because of who you are, to distort reality.

Taking the measure of the person behind the big desk in the corner office is only the beginning, however. No single individual has a world view broad enough and deep enough to produce a complete and accurate picture of reality.

A Network of Sensors

The man (or woman) who seeks to become a transleader must therefore look far beyond himself. He must develop, maintain and continuously use an extensive network of sensors—people within the organization at all levels, as well as people outside of the organization, suppliers, competitors, public officials and especially customers.

You may be getting hard facts and numbers from some of these people, but that's not what we're talking about here. We're talking about the intangible, the internal, the personal—feelings, impressions, feedback, pulse-taking, evaluating. You need these people to tell you about the health of the organization, to alert you to problems that haven't shown up in the reports and may not, to talk about their personal experiences openly and honestly.

That's the hard part—the "openly and honestly". It is all too easy to mistake a lack of complaints for evidence that nothing is wrong, when in reality, the people who were disappointed or feel mistreated are simply too disgusted or too discouraged to speak out. And most people will be happy to tell you what they think you want to hear, rather than what they actually feel.

The solution to this problem lies in the extent and the robustness of your sensor system. It also lies in the trust you are able to engender in the people you talk to, the sincerity with which you welcome any information, good news or bad. It's nice to get good news, of course, but what you're really after is bad news, and the opportunity to fix what's broken.

Connecting with Customers

No group of people is more essential to your firm's survival and success than your customers. No group of people is more worthy of your attention. You need to know how they feel about your company and its products at every moment where your paths cross, from their response to your advertising to when it's time to replace the product they bought.

The reason is obvious. In the 21st century, given the cost of recruiting new customers, you can't afford to simply sell your customer goods and services. You must sell them a relationship. You must sell them a shared experience, and one that is positive for them. The pace of change and need for adaptability is just as important to your customer as it is to you. So instead of observing how they respond to change, you have to be there in the midst of their change. 20% of transleader's time should be spent interfacing and being with the customer. The transleader must "be in the life of" the customer not just as a distant enquirer.

That means you need to know a *lot* about your customers. Most people and companies focus only on the time the consumer uses your product or service. Time is the great equalizer. Every consumer is also an individual. We each have 1440 minutes in each day. Organizations led by the transleader understand that the company needs access to how each consumer spends all of their 1440 minutes. It is understanding how subtle changes in the macro-environment effect your customers and suppliers as entities and individuals. You have to have awareness of and attention to the subtle so you can observe, adapt and respond. You need to know them not only as consumers, but also as human beings. You need to know about their hopes, their dreams, their fears. You need to know how they see themselves in relation to the world and to each other. You need to know if they like sports, how often they eat pizza, if they help their kids with homework—who they are in ways that have no direct connection to the goods or services you sell them. That's what it takes to build a real relationship. And that's a job for your network of sensors.

What do we mean by "network of sensors"? We mean people—a large, far-flung and constantly changing cast of characters with whom you are in frequent, but irregular and informal contact, people that you *see* as sensors, people whose observations and opinions you feel you can trust.

So, with this self-examination and this vast network of censors, can you now be confident that you have a pretty good handle on reality, a good grasp on the environment in which you and your organization are operating? Sorry, not quite yet.

What Outliers Can Tell You

If your goal is to be a transleader for the 21st century, several other groups of people deserve your attention—people you might be inclined to overlook, even dismiss.

The first of these are the "outliers"—the nerds, misfits and eccentrics who are to one degree or another, marching to the beat of a different drummer.

The need to belong is fundamentally more primal than the need for excellence. Outliers have chosen to be individuals. Unlike those who fit into the group smoothly and easily, outliers haven't—and probably can't—adjust themselves and their world view to match those of the majority. They are relatively isolated, which means their peers have less influence on them than is common to most other people. They have had to work harder to understand their place in the world, and their struggle is probably on-going. They're fundamentally at odds with conventional rules and views, so they're forced to rely on their intuition. As a result, Outliers have greater accuracy in their sensory perception and are interesting sources of wisdom.

This means that outliers are an extraordinary source of unconventional information, insights and ideas. Make it a practice to consider what they have to say. Even when their views are outlandish, they may well contain a grain of truth, a grain of truth you might not have encountered if you hadn't sought out the nerds, a grain of truth that can deepen your understanding of the world.[2]

Listening to Dissenters

You may also be inclined to dismiss another group, one that can be found in every organization, at almost every level: the dissenters, the champions of minority opinions, the people who think you're wrong, or that you're making a mistake. Dissent may be an essential part of their temperament, or they may have their reasons, or they may be acting out of envy.

---

2   Gladwell, Malcolm. *Outliers*, 2008.

Whatever its unconscious source, dissent is valuable to anyone who is seeking a reasonably complete and accurate view of reality. It represents another point of view and—if you let yourself consider it—it helps you reassess your own point of view, or it helps you add new information to what you already know and believe.

The trick is to entertain dissent without reflexively dismissing it, without letting your ego or your own strong opinion squash it. You have to put aside your beliefs for a time and draw out the dissenter and his or her reasons for dissent. They may or may not change your mind, but they will test your logic and your conclusions.

If you squelch dissent, or if you avoid it, you will have less reason to be confident in your conclusions. And you will have cut yourself off from what may be crucially important and significantly different views of the reality in which you think you're operating.

According to one of the insiders in Barack Obama's Presidential campaign, when he gathered his staff to solve problems or make decisions, he asked questions, but avoided signaling his preferences until the very end of the meeting. "He has a terrific poker face", the insider said. "You really don't know what he's thinking."

This technique encourages meeting participants to say what they really think, not to be yes men, and to honestly explore the alternatives. It's an effective way to avoid stacking the deck before the game is played.

Be Mindful of the Wisdom Around You

Another group of people is worth including in your search for knowledge. This one is valuable because it will give you information, not so much about the present, but about the future. These are not the people who have been where you've been, but the people who are headed where you're headed.

It is tempting—and comfortable—to surround yourself with people who've been beside you in past, who've faced the same risks, worked the same hours, struggled with the same doubts. You know them, they know you.

But these may not be the people you want or need beside you during the next phase. They may be exhausted, discouraged, or simply finished fighting. They may not have enough energy or enthusiasm for the next transformation.

You may find these new people among your younger staff members—the ones who have grown up with technological change and are comfortable with society as it is now—diverse, individualistic and international.

It will serve you well if you identify those who share your vision and your drive. Their spirit will nourish yours and vice versa. And they will see things that you need to see.

When Enough is Enough

Now, after all this talk about information seeking and getting the clearest possible picture of reality, we're going to look at the other side of the coin. You cannot hope to know and absorb all of the information that comes your way, to know everything about the business environment. If you try, you will fail. It is endless.

So you must apply a filter to the information that surrounds and bombards you. Ask yourself: *Is this relevant?* If it's not, you need to ignore it, so you'll have the time and the energy to deal with what *is* relevant.

What we're suggesting is not that you try to know everything. We're suggesting that you start with a broad view, but quickly decide what's relevant and seek the deepest possible information about your organization and what relates to it. It's a depth vs. width issue, and we think transleaders should be going after depth, not just width.

We are talking about the type of observatory skills that can survey the landscape with a flexible and powerful lens that has the ability to zoom in and zoom out and view from several vantage points and perspectives is. Another way to look at this is to see the Earth from an astronaut's point of view or to log on to Google Earth and see exactly where you are. You have to know what's out there. Knowing when to truly take more time and observe at a deeper level will be required in this new economy. The practice of going from one-foot depth to ten-foot depth requires higher levels of skill, practice and discipline. After you've done your survey, it's time to look at what's truly relevant, at the deeper level. What we're talking about here is human capacity. No one can know everything. So you must concentrate on the areas that are truly relevant to you. That's what's going to improve your chances for success.

The transleader knows that his or her time and energy are limited, and therefore must not be wasted, but used with skill and wisdom. This doesn't apply only to information coming at you from the outside. It also applies to internal paperwork and email.

The ease of email, especially, has led many employees to send copies to others indiscriminately, not because the others needed the information, but because the emailer wanted to impress others with his or her activity, or to assert involvement that didn't really exist. This results in email inboxes that are stuffed not with obvious spam, but with irrelevant data masquerading as something important.

Several corporations have handled this dilemma by revolutionizing their internal communications. They have practically outlawed email, in favor of instant messaging. Instant messaging is almost always the result of genuine activity and necessary interaction. Also, it's difficult to save, which means it doesn't leave a paper trail. So keeping email (and attachments) to the barest minimum means a net increase in executive time and energy.

To be a transleader, you have to set up systems and filters like this in order to keep relevant information flowing smoothly, and to reduce the time wasted reviewing copies of memos and reports that may have some value to their senders, but none to you. It's the kind of informational discipline that can easily add significant time to your day. From a business point of view time is inventory. Each person has a specific capacity to deploy brilliance. Once that wattage/inventory is used up, there may be a body at the computer but the brilliance isn't creating value. We have to be careful because of the time/energy perspective.

You also need to develop a sixth sense about what's wheat and what's chaff. That means learning how to prioritize your information flow, how to focus on what's meaningful and how to exclude the irrelevant. It also means resisting the urge to Google yourself to death.

Working With Others

How a CEO works with others in his organization—not just the COO, the CFO, and others at the "C level", but also people further down the pyramid—has always been a critical aspect of leadership. In the 21st century organizational environment, where talented people have all kinds of opportunities and fewer reasons for loyalty, it is even more important.

More to the point, it is important because the people you work with are all engaged, together, in something that cannot be won by one person alone. The age of the lone wolf, the corporate hero, is over. So is the age of the yes man. We are entering an era that demands *combined* effort, talent and intelligence.

In today's competitive environment, you will need your people's best efforts and to get them, you will have to move past some of what you were taught about leadership in business school, or even in your prior organizational experience. You're going to have to change, if you want to give yourself and your organization the best chance for success.

Change how?

Sharing Leadership

To put it bluntly, you're going to have to find ways to *share* leadership, to share decision-making, to share the responsibility. We know that this is a very different leadership paradigm from the one provided by conventional wisdom. According to conventional wisdom, the leader makes all of the big decisions, and keeps a close eye on the little ones too. According to conventional wisdom, the CEO may listen to what others have to say, but he or she gives the orders. According to conventional wisdom, the CEO sits behind the steering wheel and determines the course of the company. Back seat drivers are tolerated at best, and given the boot if they get out of hand. The CEO has a tough and lonely job.

In fact, the job is so tough that, as we have observed much too often, many CEOs of small-to-medium-sized corporations are working themselves into the ground—working 80 hour weeks, becoming strangers to their families, trying to do more than is humanly possible, setting themselves up for heart attacks and strokes. Nothing is worth that price.

But we're not suggesting a change in the conventional definition of leadership in order to ease your workload. We believe that if you're a CEO, the best way to assure your company's success and survival, the best way to strengthen your company, is to *share* the burdens and responsibilities of leadership with others in your organization.

The truth is, you don't have any real choice. If you want to attract and hold onto the best people, and if you want them to give you their very best efforts, you must make them genuine partners, allies and cohorts in the direction of the company. They have to feel like participants, not subordinates.

It probably won't be easy to make this change. It isn't easy to give up being an organization's absolute monarch. It's a familiar and traditional role, a role society understands and approves of. It's a comfortable position, one that provides complete clarity and total power.

People are not usually inclined to surrender power, especially if they've had to work hard to get it. And exercising it, though it has its own risks, can certainly be emotionally satisfying. But we're not asking you to give up power, at least not without compensation. We strongly believe that sharing power will put you in a position to gain even more power—not the sort of power that gives you a more secure dictatorship or intimidates your associates and employees, but the much stronger power that springs from mutual trust, mutual respect and shared goals. And it is not just increased personal power; it is increased organizational energy.

How can you know if you are actually practicing share-leadership, rather than just giving lip service to it? The clearest indicator is the appearance of leadership behavior not just in the top layer of management, but in other parts of the organization, in areas where it might not be expected or where it was lacking before. Another indicator is when you notice "I" communications diminishing and "we" communications increasing.

What must you do differently in order to achieve this level of shared leadership?

Encouraging Diverse Views

The first step is to purposely and intentionally make the decision to listen to and consider seriously diverse points of view within your organization. This means strongly encouraging others to express their views and not punishing productive disagreement. It means you must listen with an open mind.

This has two virtues: First, it provides a variety of viewpoints, which can be used to test a thesis from several different directions, engender new ideas, and point out paths to changes and improvements if necessary. Second, by giving other key executives the respect of being heard and being a part of the process, it encourages them to buy into the final decision with their whole hearts.

From encouraging dissent to working toward consensus decision-making is only a short step. Ideally, when a decision has been made, everyone in the room should feel that he or she had their say and was taken seriously. They should all feel that they played a crucial part in the decision-making and that in a very real way, the decision was theirs—everyone's.

What you're doing is building talent. You're asking your people to exceed themselves. You're taking advantage of their different perspectives and different personalities. You are making tangible your respect and your trust, raising your people's expectations of themselves.

The next step is to stand back and delegate important decisions to other key members of the team. Encourage them to use their initiative and their imaginations, and to try fresh approaches to traditional problems. Then, support their decisions. Express confidence in them. Encourage them.

Above all, don't make them feel that one mistake means the end of their careers. Failures will happen from time to time—they're inevitable. And they're quite valuable, for the lessons they teach and the resilience they build. That old saying—what doesn't kill you makes you stronger—applies to business decisions as well as every day life.

Encouraging and listening to dissent does not mean forfeiting your own role in decision-making, however. Your best adviser will always be yourself—your deepest instincts and intuition. Yes, listen to others and take them seriously, but trust your gut feeling too.

By giving your people the chance to participate in decisions and to make some on their own, you are only doing what every parent should be doing for his children: teaching independence, self-reliance, and self-confidence, all qualities that will make the entire organization stronger and more resilient.

You're also telling your people that their perspectives, their ideas and their talents are valuable to you and to the company. You're treating everyone with dignity and respect, which is essential to winning *their* full support and their full effort.

Empowering Individuality

There's really no precedent for empowerment in established corporate traditions and conventions, except for relatively feeble attempts such as flexitime, unassigned workspaces and casual Fridays. In the 21st century, employees want more than this. They are fiercely resistant to feeling like cogs in the machine, to looking, acting and behaving like everyone else. They are demanding the opportunity to be who they really are and to be appreciated for it.

They want to have a say in terms of their working style, the work hours they put into the job, and even the place they work. What is required here is a higher level of decision-making capacity. You can create parameters in which employees can truly make decisions and honor their own observations of the landscape.

Of course, people have always wanted to be treated as individuals. They've resented being reduced to a number. They've never wanted to be like IBM cards—bent, folded, spindled or mutilated. But in the 20th century, they didn't stand a chance against highly structured and very powerful organizations determined to stifle their individuality.

Times have changed, however. The simple truth is that stifling individuality is expensive. It's expensive to force or try to force people into pigeonholes and to lose the benefits of their distinctive world views and skill sets. It's expensive to require people to obey rules that exist for no intrinsic reason. It's counterproductive, especially when these people have other ideas, which will make them more comfortable and more efficient. Empower them. It will pay off on your bottom line.

Another aspect of empowering individuality is to embrace diversity. Superficiality, diversity may seem inconvenient and confusing. Dealing with differences requires effort. But it pays enormous dividends, by providing multiple perspectives, multiple experiences and multiple skills.

The key to dealing with diversity is curiosity. Curiosity leads to learning, and the more you learn, especially about people, their cultures, their backgrounds, their world views, the larger your vision can be.

Expressing or Fostering Confidence

It's not enough just to empower individuality and embrace diversity. It's not enough simply to give your people permission to work according to what makes them feel most at ease. You also have to stay out of their way and out of their space. You have to resist intruding. That means no frequent probing phone calls, no barrage of instant messages or email, no surprise "gotcha" visits.

Not intruding means not making unwelcome contact or doing unnecessary pulse-taking. It means communicating only when you genuinely *need* to communicate. It means demonstrating trust by not checking up. It's innocent until proven guilty—unless and until your employee demonstrates he or she can't be trusted to do his/her job with reasonable speed and efficiency. Then you can intrude.

So how do you keep an eye on your key people? You measure their value by results and impact, which is what you really need from them. You stop focusing on what they wear, how many hours they spend in the office and similar superficialities.

At the same time, you make it clear to your people that you're focused on their achievements and contributions, by expressing confidence in their abilities, being generous with your praise for a job well done, and by creatively rewarding them for their accomplishments and good judgment. Nothing wins loyalty or promotes effort as well as public recognition. Today, with social media you can Facebook and Tweet people in your organization to get more information on what is important to them outside of work. With all the resources available today—there is no excuse not to know your people intimately.

There are so many ways to make people feel "heard" and acknowledged. Paying as much attention to your employees as you do to your customers will give you access to ways to demonstrate your appreciation and ways to make their life easier. If people truly experience you "caring" about them, the more they will honor representing your company and keep a commitment to themselves to create reciprocal value.

When it's Separation Time

Inevitably, the time will come—no matter how well you treat your people—that some of them decide to move on. They want expanded opportunities. They're seeking new worlds to conquer. They can get more responsibility—or money—elsewhere. How should you react?

We believe the wrong reaction to this is to pull out all the stops, more money, more titles, more responsibility, to hold onto the departing employee—unless he or she is truly deserving and you've been remiss about handing out appropriate rewards and recognition.

The problem is this: When an employee says he or she is leaving, that employee has already left. The psychological commitment no longer exists. And trying to salvage it rarely works. If you do manage to convince the employee to stay, you'll probably damage his usefulness in the process. He'll never perform as he did before.

We've even suggested to CEOs that they ask new hires what they'll say in their departure speeches, what legacy they expect to leave when they move on. This has several purposes. It acknowledges that employment is not a prison and that you know that. It also shows that you have an expectation of them: that they will leave a legacy, they will have an impact they will be proud of.

We believe that it's legitimate for new people to think about leaving with a legacy—it will make them perform much more energetically. They will feel that they've made a commitment—not to stay forever, which is impossible, but to do right by their new employers, to give their best.

This kind of conversation is another acknowledgement—that you're not hiring this person because of her skill sets, especially her current skill sets. You're hiring her for her talent, aptitude, preference, capacity, inclination and motivation. You're hiring her for her soul as well as her ability.

The Shift to Informality

All of this is part of a gradual shift in organizational behavior, from tight and inflexible to loose and informal. It's part of recognizing that formality is one of efficiency's many enemies. Formality creates extra work and unnecessary constraints. It slows people down. It makes them cautious and self-conscious, and for no good reason.

Informality is the great leveler. It makes people more approachable. It encourages casual contacts and information sharing. It promotes fresh thinking. It reduces the intimidation of rank. It encourages frankness and openness. The net effect is to speed up interactions at every level, and to ratchet up organizational efficiency, not to mention making organizational ambiance friendlier and less stressful.

Responsibilities of the Transleader

In an era of shared leadership, what is the appropriate role of the CEO? Undoubtedly, the role of the person at the top is still the single most important factor in the success or failure of the organization. But in the transorganization, his skill set, his knowledge and his experience are only part of what he must supply. He must also be able to direct a network of other leaders—people scattered through the organization.

In a way, his role is more like the conductor of an orchestra and less like the violinist or the piano soloist. Ideally, he or she doesn't actually make any music, but instead makes sure that the many members of the orchestra play the same symphony, at the same tempo, in complete harmony.

The conductor has a unique position. He alone sees the orchestra, in all its sections and instruments. It is his vision of how the music should sound that must prevail. He is the one, in fact, who chooses what the orchestra should play. He's the one ultimately responsible for pleasing the audience, for choosing the instrumentalists, and for ensuring the orchestra's survival.

The conductor can't email or telephone orchestra members in mid-concert to say "faster" or "louder" or anything else. And yet a good conductor somehow manages to communicate his intentions and his vision, with great impact. And when the orchestra plays, it creates the music he was hearing in his head. How does he do this?

He uses the time available to him when the orchestra is practicing or rehearsing. He talks to the orchestra members individually. He is utterly clear about his intentions, his expectations and his values. He shares his vision, his heart and his soul, at the deepest possible level.

More than that, he takes the measure of the orchestra members. He does his best to harmonize his vision with the vision of the other players, and with the organization as a whole, with its organic identity, with how it sees itself and how it is seen by the world.

Transleaders vs. Managers

Once upon a time, if you were good at something, you had a 10-15 year window in which to employ your knowledge and skills in the service of your career and your organization. Your contributions led directly to higher profitability, to increased market share, and to operational excellence.

In those days, good CEOs were masters of incrementally improving the performance of their organizations. Business was more traditional and, without the internet and global market, CEOs had more ability to manage cause and effect. Therefore, leading relevant change in the organization was relatively less difficult. Change comprised the continuous improvement of the CEO or leader of the organization.

The greatest skill of these CEOs was focus. When they took over a company, they threw out everything they thought was irrelevant. They'd say, "We're going to focus on the one thing that will give us the greatest return." They had an excellent sense of reality. These CEOs created toolkits for themselves—quality control, just-in-time manufacturing or lean thinking. They become better at managing fixed assets. The whole concept of intangible assets and the experience economy would have never occurred to these CEOs. It was material in; product out. Profit from sales plus saving in manufacturing process.

They'd stay their 10-15 years, then move on to another organization—a bottling company, for instance—that needed better focus, productivity improvements and incremental gain. They were very alert, very competitive and very successful. But they didn't think about other things.

John Scully was a hero at Pepsi, inventing "The Pepsi Generation" and leading that company toward operational excellence. Then he went to Apple and tried to use the same toolkit. This time it didn't work. Apple required a very different perspective—because by that time, the world was changing too quickly.

By this time, it was not enough for a CEO to be a leader-manager. He or she had to be a leader-strategist. Most CEOs, even today, don't want to know how to build the machine. They want to take control of something that already exists and run it better than the last guy.

This paradigm doesn't work anymore. It is the foreman mentality, the mindset of people who accept the rules, the territory and the scope of the organization and who don't want to rock the boat.

These hands-on operational gurus have been the heroes of their country and of capitalism itself. But it's no longer enough for them to keep the machine humming. They have to initiate and navigate transformation, and that's not their inclination.

Ironically, the very quality that has made heroes of these people has diminished their capacity to be transleaders. They have learned to clear their minds, constrain their curiosity and vision and focus on the head of a pin. Sometimes we saw people who were able to solve a problem in their domain, but lacked the courage to commercialize their own domain-specific inventions and translate that to business opportunities in other areas. For example, consider a typical case where companies solve an internal problem by inventing new methods or software applications for internal use, but lack the energy and the drive to re-package that intellectual property—or product—and generate more derivative business opportunities. In today's economy, how you solve a problem becomes a product for a market.

Transleaders, by contrast, must liberate their curiosity, give full reign to their vision, and fill their minds with views from all points of the compass and act with courage. It takes a transleader to see that the "how" is as important as the "what".

If you are a manager or CEO and you want to maximize your contribution to your organization's survival and success, you have three choices. First, you transform yourself into a leader with breadth and vision, if you have the flexibility. Or you find someone within the organization with whom you can share leadership, who can provide that perspective. Or you outsource this kind of leadership to consultants or other wise men and women.

But no longer can you be content with being the best leader there is.

The Organizational Soul

We've several times mentioned the soul of your organization. Most of the time, when this subject comes up in consultations or speeches, we've found that CEOs are surprised by the idea. They don't think of their companies as having an intrinsic soul, or an internal identity beyond the public face fostered by advertising, marketing and public relations.

And yet every organization has a soul, and if it is out of harmony with the soul of the CEO or the employees, the result is a dysfunctional organization, moving or trying to move in two ore more directions at once, or part of it in motion and the rest inert.

What is the underlying soul of your organization? What is its main goal? We often hear CEOs defining their goals as becoming "market leaders"— but without clearly defining what they mean by that. Market leadership can be earned in many ways, but particularly in these three:

- **Innovators**. The organizations of innovative leaders are the first to market. They redefine product performance and solutions. But this kind of leadership faces an intrinsic problem: what do you do for an encore? Do you build a market for your product and maintain it against challenges from other players, perhaps bigger players? Do you try to repeat the achievement, creating another new product? Which way lies survival and success?

VisiCalc and Apple offer two different examples of innovative leadership—and two different organizational fates. VisiCalc tried to build and dominate a market. Apple kept innovating.

- **Visionaries**. These players really transform their industries— they do not stop with innovation. They change the mindset of entire industries and create markets that did not exist.
- **Market share leaders**. These players are not necessarily the first to market or the most innovative from the product point of view. Yet they transform their markets and capture the largest share of the profit pool by finding ways to become their customers' and their partners' first choice.

Over the years, we've frequently been surprised by how little attention is given to the term "market leadership", and how rarely CEOs, when asked about their goals, can say which of the three choices above describe their objectives.

And yet, it seems obvious that each of these sets of goals call for different strategies. And this is one reason for transleader soul-searching. It's impossible to choose a course of action—a strategy—if you don't know where you want to go.

Does your company see itself as a market leader? Or a technological leader? Or a niche-filler? Is it a steady, nose-to-the-grindstone kind of place or is it fueled by imagination and breakthroughs? Is it content with its current size or is it hungry for growth? Is it adventurous or reluctant to move beyond its comfort zone? Is it guided by tradition and history or future-oriented? How much energy does it generate?

Whatever the identity of your organization, is it in harmony with your own? If not, you may be hitting the accelerator while your organization is in neutral. That wastes time and energy and it makes progress harder and slower.

Unless you founded your organization, built it and maintained it pretty much by yourself, in line with your innermost beliefs and values, you might discover that there's a mismatch between you and your organization. If this is the case, if the organization pre-dates you, or if its identity is in conflict with yours, that's a situation that doesn't bode well for your company's success, growth or even survival.

The transleader, therefore, must be ready and willing to do an organizational soul transplant, by making clear his soul and his intent, and by bringing the rest of his organization on board, by making explicit the beliefs, values and purposes by which he intends the organization to operate.

Harmonizing Souls

We believe that one of the transleader's most important tasks is to make sure there is harmony between him, the organization, and the company employees. Anything less promotes conflicts and weakens commitments.

The most effective way to do this is to consciously *model* the way—to act as you want others to act, with openness and clarity, with flexibility, with a willingness to experiment and take risks, with a tolerance for dissent, with the sharing of power, with a dedication to the truth, keeping promises and commitments and expecting the same from others, and exercising imagination and inventiveness, in an organization that operates in harmony with itself and its people.

Harmonizing your soul with the soul of the organization and its people is an essential aspect of transleadership. This is the way to get your organization truly working together, meshing as a team, sharing goals and motivations.

Consider your key people, for instance. Are their souls in harmony with yours? Do they share your goals or just pay lip service to them? Do they operate with the same sense of urgency you do? Do they share your enthusiasm? Your sense of mission? Your ambition? Your hopes? Your sense of purpose?

You're unlikely to find any clones among them, and that's good. Each can contribute his or her perspective, both to everyday operations and new ventures. And each has his or her distinctive personality and character. But your organization can't be at its maximum strength or operate at maximum efficiency unless there is harmony between you and your key people at a very deep level, and achieving that starts with openness and honesty, both *from* you and *to* you. And that's not easy. It can only happen if your people truly trust you. Building that trust depends on how you react when you hear things you don't like. If you can hear negatives without killing the messenger, you'll be going a long way.

Some of your people will already be in harmony with you. You'll hear it, you'll feel it and you'll see it. Others can be brought into the fold. They can be convinced and converted. But some will be irretrievably out of step—some won't want to change, and others won't be able to.

It may be that the disharmonious few occupy positions that are pretty self-contained, or far enough away from the main action that they can't do much harm. But if they're part of the core team and they show no signs of coming around, they may have to go. It won't do to have *almost* everyone on the team pulling in the same direction. You need basic unanimity.

It's important to keep this in mind during the recruitment process. Interview questions that elicit information about the job seeker's values, motivations and goals will help you determine whether he or she is in harmony with you and with the organization.

What do you lose if your people and your organization are not in harmony? You lose time, you lose effectiveness, you lose full utilization, you lose that most valuable of organizational commodities, energy—at the price of more conflict. You also lose the ability to connect relevant skills with the right people, and to change your own role when needed.

Twenty Steps Toward Transleadership

1. Reboot your search for truth and reality
2. Start your self-inventory
3. Establish a network of sensors
4. Communicate directly with your customers
5. Build a bridge to outliers
6. Listen to dissenters
7. Associate with the right people
8. Focus on relevant information only
9. Share important decisions with your key people
10. Nurture under-utilized pools of leadership in your organization
11. Encourage diverse views
12. Treat your employees as adults
13. Empower your team's individuality
14. Reward your people appropriately
15. Embrace the movement toward informality
16. Figure out how you can increase your impact at a distance
17. Make explicit the soul of your organization
18. Harmonize your soul with the souls of your key people
19. Model the behavior you want to see in others
20. Let yourself become the conductor, not a musician.

Part Seven—Your Personal Transformation

*He who has done his best for his own time has lived for
all times.*
Friedrich Schiller

We've talked a lot about how organizations and leaders need to change to align themselves with the 21st century, with today's business environment. We've described at length what it takes to create a transorganization or be a transleader.

We believe you cannot hope to become a transleader and guide a transorganization without a clear life goal, without a balanced personal life, without self-esteem, without good communication skills, without good work habits, and without a strongly developed sense of personal responsibility. These are the foundation blocks on which everything else is built.

Your Life Goal

It is all too easy to forget, as you immerse yourself in daily events and struggles, as you try to find time to read books about leadership, as you deal with an email inbox, a smart phone, and an answering machine full of problems, not to mention the people lined up outside your office, that you underlie all of this.

Ultimately, *you* are the person to whom you're accountable. You are accountable for how you spend your time. You are accountable for what you achieve.

This raises questions worth considering:

- What is your long-term life goal?
- What steps are you taking, right now, to achieve that?
- What behaviors move you toward your goals?
- What behaviors—in yourself—do you most admire?
- What aspects of your life should become habitual and characteristic of you?

- Which of your past accomplishments helps you most with current issues?

You are also accountable to the other people in your life, your family, friends and associates. Every responsible and aware adult should also understand that they do nothing in isolation. They leave fingerprints on everything they do. They influence everyone with whom they come into contact.

- How do you hope to influence family, friends and co-workers?
- What do you do that is worthy of emulation by others?
- What do you want to leave in your wake? Chances are, if you haven't figured that out, if you're not striving for it, if you haven't made it one of your goals, there's no telling what you'll be leaving behind...

All of these questions deserve answers, and it's not a one-time process. They deserve consideration whenever you go through important changes, whenever you move from one stage of life to the next. A good way to remind yourself is to keep a daily journal. And, every year or so, read it from the beginning.

Of course, there are no self-reflection police. No one will know if you don't take the time to think about your life this way—except you. But, as we've said, you are accountable to yourself.

Personal Life

The press of business, the responsibilities of leadership, the problems and obstacles you focus on—all this and more can make you forget where your strength comes from and distract you from taking care of yourself.

But the simple fact is that you can't take care of business if you don't first take care of yourself. These are the areas to watch out for:

- Your health—your physical well-being: sleep, exercise, nutrition, medical care. Don't cheat yourself. Get what you need. This is why flight attendants tell you to put the oxygen mask on yourself first if there is an emergency. It isn't thoughtless or selfish. It merely gives you the power to help others and take care of yourself.

- Your spirituality—your conviction that you and your life matter. It isn't enough to make assumptions or to ignore this aspect of your life. Your belief in yourself is what gives you the power to choose your future. It requires nurturing.

- Your relationships—good relationships with your spouse and children, healthy long-term satisfying intimacies, a rich and full social life. When something is wrong here, it's as though you have a hole in your pocket, out of which is leaking critical supplies of energy and self-confidence.

- Your emotional well-being—your ability to embrace your talent without pride and your inadequacies without shame.

- Your finances—a foundation that gives you psychological safety. If you're operating hand-to-mouth, you're putting energy where it doesn't belong. You need to do whatever it takes to fix the problem.

- Your intellect—a vibrant curiosity about the world and a strong and continuing interest in work, in the future, in art, culture, literature, entertainment and everything else that keeps the mind active and alive.

If your life is in good shape in all of these areas, you're ready to take on greater leadership responsibilities and to work at the peak of your powers. But to the extent that something needs attention, you'll be at less than optimal strength.

Skill Development

Thanks to the nature of life, learning is a lifelong process if you're paying attention, whether or not you are actively pursuing knowledge. Without goals or focus, however, learning is haphazard and accidental. For people who occupy leadership roles, or are seeking them, this is less than ideal.

It is our contention that leaders or potential leaders—in fact, just about everyone—should be learning by *intention*, through the adoption of a set of very clear objectives and habits.

We believe everyone should develop three skills simultaneously and continue sharpening them until they've been mastered. Then ask for 360-degree feedback to make sure you've accomplished what you think you have. Then find more skills to master, one in each of these areas:

1. Job-related—a skill directly related to your current position, part of your company's review process.
2. Business-savvy—a skill that allows you to better understand the bigger picture—systems thinking, lean thinking, blue ocean strategy.
3. Interpersonal—a skill involving improved teamwork, leadership, emotional or social intelligence.

Self-Esteem

It's very hard, if not impossible, to accomplish much if you don't begin with a certain amount of self-esteem or self-confidence. Lack of self-esteem leads to confusion, uncertainty, fear, doubt, and, in the worst cases, self-destructive behavior—if you believe that you don't have much worth, then you will also believe that you don't deserve much. Self-esteem problems can be the result of either nature or nurture or a combination of the two. According to some theories, individuals can be hard-wired to have low self-esteem. According to others, problems with self-esteem often have roots in childhood, with perfectionist or over-demanding parents.

Low self-esteem can even affect people who have a long list of tangible reasons for self-esteem—lifelong records of accomplishment, kindness, generosity, helping others. Adult failures can also contribute, whether they are in a person's private life or his or her working life.

A shortfall in self-respect has serious consequences in many areas of life. It can make you self-doubting, passive, easily dominated by others, reluctant to express a strong point of view, hesitant to ask for well-earned compensation or status, afraid to demand good treatment, even love. It can lead to depression and even paralysis.

If you're suffering from low self-esteem, you probably know it all too well. But if you're in doubt, try this: would you befriend yourself? Would you hire you, knowing you as you do? Would you enjoy hanging out with you? Do you have to admit, in all modesty, that you're a pretty neat person? Do you trust you, admire you, laugh at your jokes? If you can honestly answer "yes" to these questions, your self-esteem is probably in pretty good shape.

If not, however, you are among the many, many people whose self-esteem could use burnishing. It is not easy to overcome childhood disapproval, even with psychotherapy. And failure on the job or in your personal life certainly takes its toll. But it is possible to build an intellectual bulwark against low self-esteem, based on objective evaluations of past and current events and on an acknowledgement of the qualities all human beings share.

As for the objective evaluation, the odds are high that if you look honestly at your life, you'll find that you've been a pretty decent human being, apart from the usual share of human failings. And if you feel you're thin on virtues, this is an excellent time to begin accumulating them. Nothing is as effective at making you feel good about yourself as doing good for others, and giving time and energy works much better than giving money.

But there is another reason for self-esteem, one that transcends good character and good deeds: your humanity. Your deepest self. Your soul. This entitles you to believe that, in the big picture, you matter. You have value. You can authentically make any and all of the following statements:

- I am
- I can
- I will
- I want
- I desire
- I think
- I feel

All of these statements indicate an unquenchable selfhood, a level of consciousness and awareness that goes beyond the details of your life. Understanding the truth in those statements is one of the prerequisites of success. It is an enormously empowering insight.

The belief that you matter is what gives you the motivation and the ability to consider all of your potential, to listen to the wisdom within you and to make the choices that will guide your life in a positive direction. It allows you to take responsibility for yourself.

Personal Responsibility

Taking responsibility for yourself is not like flipping a light switch. There are levels and degrees. There's ignoring the idea, taking a stab at it and committing to it. We've divided it into eight levels:

1. *I am unaware and unconscious.*
   This describes the mental life of an animal, a very low animal, the kind that operates entirely by instinct and habit. If this describes you, anything good that happens to you is an accident, likewise anything bad. But in a world of constant and unexpected change, your odds of survival are much less than those of beings who can think and act with conscious intent.

2. *I blame and complain.*
   This is just a way of proclaiming powerlessness. It's a way of saying "What happens to me is not my fault". But this is profoundly untrue. You are capable of action. You're just denying it. In that sense, you're deceiving yourself. You're not seeing reality. And you're certainly not taking responsibility for yourself.

3. *I make excuses.*
   Well, you're thinking, anyhow—you're looking at your problem with a certain amount of rationality. But you're surrendering all of your power to some outside entity—government, management, spouse, parent, etc. The truth is that if you're willing to accept it, you have the power over what happens to you. But you have to accept it and put it to use.

4. *I hope and wait.*

   Hope is neither a strategy nor a plan. It relies not on individual action, but on external events. It short-circuits personal accountability. Hope is a kind of limbo. It means you're not unhappy enough to complain and not happy enough to act. In some circumstances, it can be momentarily reassuring, but it can also be paralyzing. It is a lure to inaction. A plan, any plan, is better than unadorned hope. And hope does not rise to the level of personal responsibility.

5. *I acknowledge reality.*

   Well, that's certainly a start. But many people refuse to do that. They feel impelled to be pessimists—things will turn out badly; or optimists—things will turn out well. Neither of these is reality. Reality means anything is possible, and that your future is in your hands.

6. *I "own" it.*

   You are the creator of every outcome in your life. If it's miserable, you own it. If it's delightful, you own it. Admitting that you own the outcomes in your life is another way of saying that you have the power to change it.

7. *I seek solutions.*

   There is no problem that doesn't have a solution. But many people won't accept solutions they don't like. And many people imply that they're seeking solutions, but they're only paying lip service to the idea. Truly seeking solutions means whole-heartedly focusing on the problem at hand and not giving up until you've conquered it.

8. *I make it happen.*

   The brilliance from Yoda (the archetypal sage from Star Wars) taught us, "There is no try, only do." When you make a commitment to a specific outcome, getting there requires right thought and right action. It also requires genuine determination. Nothing less will do it. This is taking personal responsibility at the deepest level. It is your best chance to create your own future.

Relationship/Communications Skills

Perhaps the key relationship skill, in business and in the rest of your life, is to be able to communicate with others effectively, productively and empathetically.

People engage in all kinds of conversations—utilitarian conversations, loving conversations, friendly conversations, and a dozen different varieties of small talk. Most of these do not involve conflict, which means that they are not inherently tricky.

The tricky ones involve what might euphemistically be called "an exchange of views". These can happen a dozen times a day, at work or in every other area of life, and they often turn out either as win-win encounters or lose-lose encounters.

This is how they become lose-lose.

- One person makes a statement. The second disagrees— *before communicating differences.* The outcome: the first person feels disrespected and may end up with negative feelings toward the second. At the same time, the second undervalues the potential contribution of the first person, and likewise come away with negative feelings.

- One person makes a statement. The second immediately *defends* his point of view and pays little attention to the first person's point of view, failing to learn anything from it. Each ends up feeling negative toward the other.

In both cases, the relationship is damaged and the chances for successful interaction in the future are diminished, because the odds of more lose-lose encounters are increased. This is a cycle of waste.

But there is another way to conduct this kind of conversation, one that leads to a win-win result and encourages more of them. It's based on three concepts:[3]

1. **Align:** Undertake conversations with the intent that they create shared purpose, stimulate creativity, and ensure smart planning.

---

3   Connolly & Rianoshek. *The Communication Catalyst*, 2002 (p.19-20).

2. **Act:** Conduct conversations with the intent of clarifying accountabilities and launching action.

3. **Adjust:** Have conversations that review results and translate the experience into improvement.

Missing from this, you'll note, are disagreements, defences and damage. They're missing by intent. They're missing because one of the parties to the conversation, if not both of them, made the conscious choice to avoid them.

Win-win interaction is a matter of chance without authentic listening—a deep awareness of what's going on when two people are talking to each other, and a dedication to genuine communication.

But people have various reasons for conversations, and sometimes honesty is not among them.

- If they're trying to avoid difficulties, they often rely on *pretence*—lying, withholding information, giving answers or statements that are in direct conflict with each other. People do this because they think it's an effective way to protect themselves or the other person. Either way, pretence is a step backward from reality and it is a signal of mistrust. One way to decrease this kind of behavior is to make the person you're talking with feel safe, safe enough to speak honestly.

- If they're defending their honest position, they may be entirely *sincere*—but they may exhibit a thoughtless certainty that their view is accurate. You won't be able to change their mind if you don't listen to and honor their position. But you must also be open to the possibility that yours is the mind that should change. The aim is to see reality.

- If they're simply conveying information and comparing facts, *accuracy* is the guiding principal. But truly accurate observations must include the possibility that perceptions may not be reality. Only real-life testing can confirm them.

- If their aim is to clarify essential purposes and identity paths to action, then the guiding principle should be *authenticity*. In authentic conversations, there is a mutual and genuine appreciation of all views, and all factors, a genuine striving for insights and a genuine search for opportunity.

It's this last type of interaction that promotes trust, efficiency and clarity—all of which are important factors in both personal and organizational success.

Work Habits

Everyone has a fixed number of watts of energy, although that number varies from person to person. It's the amount of energy you have before you are completely exhausted, before you lose concentration, before you can no longer trust your own thinking process, before you can no longer refuse your mind and body's demands for rest.

That fixed amount of energy is related to time, to hours of work, but it is not the same. Intensity, pressure, multiple problems, interruptions, difficult working conditions, multiple meetings, extra personnel, physical and mental health and many other conditions are all factors that may affect energy levels.

But most people tend to act as though time and energy are one and the same. So, if they work longer hours, they expect their efforts to add value in the same proportion as working only regular hours. This is exactly like the person who insists he must still have money in the bank because he hasn't used all the checks in his checkbook.

A growing body of research supports the idea that extra hours on the job do not provide extra value or lead to a greater number of accomplishments. In fact, studies show that the extra hours have a negative effect on the quality of work and the quality of life away from work. Extra hours lead to diminished energy during regular hours. So when you work overtime or cut back on sleep so you can work more, what you're really doing is stealing the wattage you need for your family, yourself and even your normal work activities.

This is one of the most common problems in our society today. In the effort to be supermen and women, we are deriving ourselves of sleep, we are depriving ourselves of quality family time, and we are depriving ourselves of time for thought and genuine relaxation. We are doing a terrible job at managing our energy at the very moment we are feeling proud about giving up another half-hour of sleep.

The people who do this are telling themselves that they don't have the usual human limitations or needs. They think they are demonstrating their superior endurance or strength or determination, but the truth is they are undermining themselves and diminishing their ability to contribute.

In a Harvard Business Review article, "Manage Your Energy, Not Your Time", Tony Schwartz and Catherine McCarthy outlined a rational plan to help people maximize the amount of productive energy they could make available in the business environment.

They looked at the four different sources of personal energy and figured out how simple changes and improvements in awareness could replenish it and keep it topped up:

Physical Energy

Don't cheat on sleep. Do cardiovascular exercises at least three times a week. Instead of eating big, infrequent meals, eat small meals and snack on something healthy every three hours or so.

Learn to notice when your energy level is flagging. It produces obvious symptoms: restlessness, yawning, difficulty focusing. These are all signs that it's time to take a break.

And, whether or not it fits into your "schedule", get up from your desk or otherwise stop doing what you're doing every hour-and-a-half or two and walk around the block, or have a brief, pleasant, non-business conversation with a colleague. Consider these breaks debts to yourself that must be paid on time.

Emotional Energy

Emotions have a powerful effect on personal energy. They can either drain it or multiply it. How can you minimize the drain and maximize the multiplication? Schwartz and McCarthy propose three answers:

First, defuse negative emotions, such as irritability, anxiety, insecurity and impatience. The first part of defusing is to recognize, objectively, what you are feeling. The second part is interrupting the flow with a solid 1-3 minutes of deep abdominal breathing.

Second, fuel positive emotions in yourself and others by expressing appreciation and admiration in detail, in more than a perfunctory "thank you". Don't be a phoney, but choose incidents and achievements that other people have genuine reason to be proud of.

Third, when you find yourself in an uncomfortable or unpleasant situation, try looking at it through a different lens. If it's a personal conflict, put yourself in the shoes of the other person. Look at the situation through the other person's eyes. Or ask yourself this: "How will I view this in six months? Will I even remember it six months from now?"

Both of these are detachment techniques, designed to interrupt the negative thoughts, to put your emotions on hold and to give you the opportunity to contemplate the situation intellectually. Both techniques are quite useful.

Mental Energy

Distractions are the most ubiquitous and persistent energy wasters in the business environment. But there are common sense ways to minimize the worst of their species. We're talking about email and the telephone.

Technique #1: When you're working on a job that requires high concentration or intense focus, find yourself a place as far from phones and email as possible. Or temporarily disconnect your phone and pull the plug on the Internet. Make it as inconvenient for yourself as possible to yield to the temptation to check your email or answer your phone.

Technique #2: Designate specific times during the day—say 11am and 4pm.—to check your email and consider it forbidden at any other time, emergencies aside.

The fourth source of personal energy mentioned in the article, namely "The Human Spirit", is in fact an element of what we presented here as the third pillar of future leadership—the Soul—and the ability to harmonize your own soul with the soul of your organization. Clearly, once you do that, it will be a huge source of energy.

When you have absorbed and made habits out of the lessons here, in terms of your life goals, your personal life, your skill development, your self-esteem, your personal responsibility, your communications skills and your work habits, you can feel confident that you have a good foundation for transforming yourself.

Part Eight: The Next Transformation

Knowing others is intelligence; knowing yourself is wisdom.
Mastering others is strength; mastering yourself is true power.
Tao Te Ching (The Wisdom of the Tao)

As we've seen, the megatrends of the late 20th and early 21st century have given birth to the transorganization—a new way of doing business, a new way of competing in the world marketplace, a new kind of home for employees, and requiring a new kind of organizational leadership.

But the world is continuing to change, and faster than ever. New forces, new megatrends—global megatrends—are appearing on the horizon that threaten to make life even harder for traditional organizations, while simultaneously accelerating the growth of transorganizations and pushing them toward even greater change.

The current global economic environment is likely to delay the advent of at least some of these megatrends, but their eventual arrival is almost inevitable. And understanding them and their relevance to business and organizations of almost every other kind will be critical to every leader and CEO.

As global citizens and incurable optimists, we have long been fascinated by humanity's possibilities. We think our species has made significant progress in recent years, and we believe that this phenomenon will only increase as the 21st century wears on.

With that in mind, we looked at the social, technological, organizational and human progress we're now experiencing, with the intent of identifying and analyzing the key forces that will shape and shake our lives in the years to come. We were motivated not only by our intellectual curiosity, but by the belief that, to succeed in the decades to come, business leaders need to tie their organizations to one or more of the megatrends that will dominate our lives.

The result of our investigation was a distillation of the most likely key trends. In all, we identified 16 of them. For the sake of clarity, we divided them into four categories: economic, geopolitical, organizational and technological. By sheer coincidence, most of these megatrends were associated with words that begin with "C". So we call them "C-changes".

In the last few years, we have presented this list of C-changes to hundreds of organizations around the world, and always with a question: Are any of these megatrends relevant to you?

In almost all cases, the answer was "yes". Actually, it was more than just "yes". It was "yes" with the surprise that comes from discovering something obvious when pointed out, but invisible until then.

Let's look at the "C-changes" category by category:

Economic Megatrends

1. **Consumers.** If the 20th century was the century of producers, the 21st is the century of consumers. There are three reasons:

   □ Until the closing decades of the 20th century, consumers had to be satisfied with the essentially identical products of industrialization. But technological developments have made possible individualization and customization, and customers are demanding no less.

   □ Today, 50% of the world's population regularly consumes products and services. But in the next 20 or 30 years, this number will grow significantly. In our lifetimes, we are likely to see an international consumer base not of a little over three billion people, but of five or six billion—the result of emerging markets that are beginning to distribute capital to those to whom it was not previously available. These phenomena will resume when the economy turns around. These numbers alone will empower consumers to get what they ask for.

   □ With the rise in the numbers of consumers, we will also see a rise in their diversity, since many of them will be coming from countries and cultures that did not engage in consumerism. This means that the new consumers will have different needs, desires and consumption habits than the existing group. This will post a significant challenge to vendors: to understand how customers plan to consume products and services. Vendors will have to constantly analyze these consumers' behavior patterns, not to mention the behavior patterns of upcoming generations.

2. **Cities, Urbanization and Crime.** Population analysts believe that the coming decades will see a worldwide and accelerated migration from rural and agricultural communities to urban and suburban areas. This means a significant rise in the number of cities with populations of 5, 10 and even 20 million inhabitants. That means trouble for municipal leaders and for the business entities that service metropolitan areas. It has serious implications in terms of quality of life, environmental issues, transportation and most of all, crime.

3. **Challengers.** For a very long time, we've all lived in a world with the old familiar economic superpowers. Yet at the turn of the 21st century, we started to see how that balance of power is changing, with the emergence of the bric club (Brazil, Russia, India, China). The wealth, productivity and creativity of these challengers is going to shift and dilute the familiar power of the 20th century economic empires. One of the most significant challenges of this realignment means that traditional Western economic powers will have to learn to collaborate—instead of trying to dominate—the rising new economies of the East. And as we look at the decades ahead, we may see further new emerging economies—in Africa and the Middle East. The West will have an even bigger challenge and will have to continuously learn how to collaborate.

4. **"Capitasocialism".** The struggle between capitalism and socialism shaped the 20th century, to a large extent. It ended with the fairly clear victory of liberal capitalism, and its acceptance as the major driving force of economic growth. However, the economic problems that began in September 2008 will hasten the already growing synthesis between these competing economic philosophies, the result

of the worldwide progress of underdeveloped countries and the need to provide the emerging middle class in these nations with a greater share of the global wealth.

5. **"Contentucation".** The 20th century was an era dominated by machinery, equipment and tangible assets. The 21st century will have a growing number of content marketplaces, which will produce knowledge, entertainment and data of all kinds. There are three major reasons for that:

☐ More and more people will need and demand *new* knowledge about *new* domains and consumers. Legacy knowledge bases and domain expertise will be less important and less valuable.

☐ The coming decades will accelerate the trend toward a longer human lifespan, which means that there will be a growing pool of leisure-oriented people who will have increased needs for knowledge and entertainment content.

☐ Shorter career cycles—the product of rapidly-changing technology—will increase the working population's need and desire for re-training and re-education, much of it in new disciplines. That means the demand for knowledge and content will grow significantly in the coming years.

Geopolitical Megatrends

1. **Community Coalitions.** The 20th century saw the rise of the nation state. In the 21st century, we are seeing the rise of communities and coalitions of nation states, acting together, harmonizing policies, unifying markets, etc. The EU is one example. Others include NAFTA (the North American Free Trade Association), OPEC and NATO. We expect other areas in the world to join in regional communities of nations, in which the individual nation states have lesser degrees of autonomy.

2. **Cross-Cultural Civilizations.** The days when single ethnic or racial groups dominated nations are quickly fading away. As a result of international freedom of movement, mobility

of talent, globalization and a variety of other economic forces, diversity is increasing throughout the world. This is a fact of life today in most of the world's open societies, although it is much less true in closed regions. The result has been two kinds of conflicts, the first between open and closed societies, the second within open societies.

Reducing the cultural and religious conflicts within open societies depends on an acceptance of the new diversity by all groups, especially the latest arrivals. The conflicts between open and closed societies are less tractable. As a result, it is vital for the open societies to prevent the use of nuclear, biological and chemical weapons by de-legitimizing extreme leaders and helping to modernize under-developed and under-privileged societies.

While it is clear that cross-cultural conflicts will continue for many years to come, we believe that they also offer many opportunities to establish economic and geopolitical bridges between the highly diverse network of communities, and that the concept of a global village may become a reality.

3. **Counter Terrorism**. We believe that global terrorism, whether based on ideology, religion or simply crime, is in the process of giving birth to a worldwide backlash. The result, we think, will be vastly increased cooperation among nations and regional communities in fighting this problem, including those nations for which the threat is largely internal.

Technological Megatrends

1. **Clean sustainability.** The energy-consuming nations have talked about breaking their oil addiction for at least 30 years, but there are strong signs that the talk is about to be replaced by vigorous action. Several factors have come together to make clean, sustainable energy a top priority, including the potential political instability of the suppliers, the growing determination of the consuming nations to protect themselves from the whims of the producing nations, the worldwide financial downturn, and, perhaps most importantly, the spectre of global warming.

In the coming decades, the industrial nations will be investing heavily in clean and sustainable energy and its associated technologies, and, as a by-product, creating a vast new employment sector. These changes will have an enormous impact on the way we live and the way we conduct business.

2. **"CompuBio".** We anticipate that the combination of digital and computing technology with advances in biological knowledge will result in new paradigms for the prevention, diagnosis and treatment of many diseases and disabilities. We also expect this new technology to produce great advances in effective nutrition and in dealing with mental disorders. In combination, we expect this to result in a longer life and better health for individuals, families and communities.

We also believe that new developments in personalized medication, dynamic medication and one-of-a-kind treatments will change the way medical services are delivered and consumed. This convergence of bio-tech and digital computing is likely to ameliorate some of the fundamental problems of healthcare which appear to be beyond solution today.

3. **"Compactization" and Convergence.** It is almost a cliché to note that the computing power in the cell phones that hundreds of millions of people carry in their pockets every day significantly exceeds the computing power of the Apollo capsule that carried three men to the moon. Or from another view of progress, the first IBM personal computers, which came to market in the mid-1980s, retailed for about $3,000 and weighed 35 pounds. Today's mobile devices provide far more functionality at a fraction of the cost and weight.

The phenomena that have made this possible is compactization and convergence. Shrinking the size of electronic devices and combining multiple functionalities in one piece of equipment is transformational. It greatly accelerates market penetration and it empowers those who could not afford or understand this technology. This challenges profit-making institutions to make full use of the powers available and offers all kinds of opportunities to those that understand the marketplaces that are emerging as a result of technological advances.

4. **Condensed cycles.** Elsewhere in the book, we've discussed how technology is compacting and condensing what we long took for granted as the natural length of a business or career cycle—20 years, more or less. We traced its shrinkage to 15 years, then 10 and it is now heading even lower. This is just a taste of what's to come. In the coming years, the cycles will come so fast that they'll start tumbling over one another. The organizations that manage to keep up with them, with a constant infusion of new talent and continuous retraining, will survive and thrive. The organizations that do not will disappear.

Business Megatrends

Many of the business trends that first appeared in the last couple of decades will become much stronger in the years to come, making it increasingly difficult to conduct business in the traditional way and more and more necessary to adopt transorganizational principles. It's important to look at these trends not only in regard to their impact on organizational life today, but in the future.

1. **Connected and Flat.** As we've already pointed out, transorganizations are far less hierarchical than traditional organizations. They operate much more as a virtual network, in part because of the networking technology that is rapidly spreading through the business world.

   In the future, hierarchical organizations will seem—and will *be*—outdated, because they will be nowhere near as nimble as their flatter cousins. The organizations of the 21st century will be constructed with highly porous borders between departments and functions, making the flow of ideas, initiatives and cooperation much easier. Companies will be structured more like communities, and less like military organizations.

2. **"Co-Acting".** In earlier chapters, we've discussed the value of shared leadership. It is a great way to strengthen an organization, to extend its perspective and improve its bench strength. This is one of the key elements in a transorganization. In the future, it may be hard to attract top-notch talent without offering a very real stake in the decision-making process and its outcome, as employees will demand no less.

   Co-Acting is more than just a trend of business practice. It is a variety of group behavior based on collective skills and intelligence, leveraging people in combination rather than individually. This type of behavior will become more and more important in the years to come, as one of the keys to organizational success. At the same time, it will require a major shift in leadership attitudes, an understanding that the organization is crucially dependent on external and internal cooperation and partnership.

3. **"Communiting".** As the 21st century wears on, an organization's ability to grow—or even to survive—will depend on its relationship with its community. An important aspect of this is encouraging team members to be active in the community. This isn't so much because it's good public relations to be socially responsible—although it certainly is that. It's because the experience an organization's people gain by being involved with their communities is extremely valuable. It allows people to develop leadership, initiative and entrepreneurship. Many of these skills translate directly into business operations.

4. **"Customerizing".** Because of the major trend toward consumerism, it is vital for organizations to develop entirely new ways of structuring organizations to take advantage of customer behaviors and expectations. This involves both product or service customizability and rapid release of new and advanced products. The companies that fail to do this, and those that provide rigid and inflexible offers, will have a hard time competing for customer interest. Clearly, the new product generations are not always offering "new functionality"—sometimes they offer only a new experience,

and sometimes they address the customers' need to buy and portray—through a product—a certain social position. Companies who want to hold the market will find, again and again, creative ways to sell the same basic functionality but with a new experience. Gillette razors are a good example of how this can be done. Every year or two, the company brings out a new and improved product that supposedly offers more to the customer and, not so incidentally, makes obsolete the previous offering, as well as competitive products.

5. **"Continusensing".** In the new marketplace, the behaviors and priorities of customers, partners, co-actors and competitors are changing faster than ever. That means it's not enough for an organization to periodically survey the competitive environment. It must constantly sense and measure information, and assess it to see if action is required.

    This new skill—the ability to continuously sense relevant signals from the outside world—will prove increasingly essential for organizations that recognize the need to understand the business environment. And a good sensory system, by itself, is not enough. It must function in real time, providing information as it happens, so that the organization can respond quickly and intuitively.

    In addition, organizations will need to develop fast reaction and fast analytical capabilities, in order to automate the assessment of risks, opportunities and fundamental shifts in consumer behavior.

    To achieve real-time "continusensing", organizations will have to develop the ability to continuously understand their interactions with the external world, and not just on the mechanical level. They will have to deeply understand these interactions on the human, content and meaning level. This is a daunting task. Imagine the effort it will take to automatically analyze and understand customer phone calls, voice interactions, web interactions and written instructions — all in real time! Every organization that attempts to acquire this skill will be challenged by the effort, but for those that succeed, it will provide an unmatched ability to instantly respond to any change that comes along.

We hope and expect that as you read about these megatrends, you asked yourself which is relevant to your business, what effect it might have and how you plan to address it.

Part Nine: Toward I-Organizations (2010-onward)

*Live your questions now, and perhaps even without knowing it,
you will live along some distant day into your answers.*
Rainer Maria Rilke

In our considered view, transorganizations—while clearly a new organizational paradigm—are yet another organizational generation, a temporary phenomenon, simply put. They will be succeeded, and quite soon—as fast as 2012, by yet another revolutionary organizational model.

We call that model the I-Organization.

The I-Organization, we believe, will function more like a living organism than an artificial construct. It will have a body and a soul, a brain and sensors, much like a human being.

And like the transorganization, the I-Organization will dramatically change the way corporations operate. The change will affect every aspect of the organization, but more than that, it will also affect every customer and every marketplace.

As the change occurs, many of today's organizations, especially those that still operate according to the traditional P-age rules, will find themselves facing a fairly grim choice: change—radically—or die.

Those companies that have already become transorganizations will have a much clearer and shorter path to the next stage of organizational evolution. In fact, we believe that no organization will be able to become an I-organization without first being a transorganization, and the same goes for CEOs and other leaders.

In a very real sense, it is the transleaders and transorganizations of today and tomorrow, as they become more efficient and more effective, who will create the I-Organization. They will do so by better and better reframing the organizational soul—as strategy builders, by making a more consistent impact from a distance, by developing a natural tendency to drive work in spontaneous coalitions and with deeper and broader shared leadership behavior.

Gradually, transorganizations will complete the organizational phase that called them into existence and become true I-Organizations.

Why "I"? Because so many of the characteristics of the I-Organization happen to begin with that letter—another one of those happy coincidences. At any rate, I-words will be the prevailing lingo of the next step in organizational evolution, highlighting fundamental shifts in several dimensions—leadership, external core competence, internal core competence, action styles and value systems—with words and concepts such as intuitive, integral and inspirational Leadership.

These words and concepts, we think, are worth examining:

Leadership Dimension

1. **Intuitive leadership.** In I-Organizations, there will be less and less time to formally learn and design. Navigation toward the future will have to rely on the collective intelligence and intuition of a leadership *network* that has thoroughly absorbed the concept of shared leadership. This will require a profound degree of agility.

2. **Integral leadership.** By this, we mean an integral view of all dimensions of the organization and the environment, as well as the corporate belief systems, plus the ability to navigate transformation through an integral model. To put it simply, it means maintaining the broadest possible perspective, whatever the circumstances.

3. **Inspirational leadership.** We believe that the CEO or leader of the I-Organization will be even less of a hands-on manager or concrete commander than the transleader. He or she will find that the greatest power and the greatest influence will come from the effortless inspiration that can provide the organization with better guidance and greater clarity.

External Core Competence

1. **Insightfulness.** This is the I-Organization's key core competence—the ability to extract valuable business insight from any of the organization's sensors. This could be based on read data, interpretation or analysis, or extracted from tangible transactions and unstructured interactions (especially between the organization's customers and digital interaction touch points). The ability to draw *immediate insight* from these sources is one of the factors that will turn I-Organizations into life-like entitles, thinking and acting. We are convinced, in fact, that extracting insight from organizational sensors and determining the correct action—all in real time—will be one of the core differentiators for I-Organizations.

2. **"Interactionability".** I-Organizations will live or die on the quality and efficiency of their external interactions and their ability to extract the right insight from them. This means that I-Organizations will need to perfect every type of interaction with their relevant communities, whether verbal, face-to-face or digital, whether over the phone, in the streets, on the website, in virtual spaces or in social networks. This will be another core I-Organization capability.

3. **Influence.** We believe that I-Organizations will, over time, be able to create bi-directional stimulus-response schemes with their external communities. They will develop ways to influence their respective customer communities, and, in that way, differentiate themselves from their competition and win customer loyalty. Influence-based strategies will include not just one-on-one interactions, but the heavy use of social networks, "parallel virtual spaces" and the digital universe.

Internal Core Competence

1. **Inclusivity.** I-Organizations will take welcoming and acceptance of diversity and individuality to new levels. Instead of simply dealing with it and respecting it, they will find ways to encourage it and to build on it. Diversity will become so integral to the organization that it will cease to be exceptional in any way.

2. **Informality.** Starting in the transorganization age, and more intensively in the I-Organization, there will be no time for formality and no inclination either. Formality is based on a degree of artificiality and strong emphasis on rank. But the prevailing ethos of the I-Organization will be based on openness, on equality and on a strong de-emphasis on hierarchy.

3. **Interpretation.** Another one of the I-Organization's core competencies will be the ability to clearly see and interpret organizational intent, subtext and meaning, from the highest level to the lowest, inside a department or between departments, on an individual basis or in increasingly common self-organized groups.

In the coming age of the I-Organization, social factors and other trends will lead people to seek employment based more on working environment than on their specific domain expertise. I-Organizations will respond by providing working environments that people of all kinds will find conducive, inviting and comfortable.

Action Styles—The Instinct-Based I-Organization

Biological entities survive on the combination of instincts and learned behavior. I-Organizations, which will have many of the characteristics of living things, will base their actions and operations on a similar combination.

But of course, since Mother Nature is not directly involved in the creation of organizations, their instincts are not built into their genes, except metaphorically. They must develop a set of protective instincts and practice them until they become instant and automatic reactions to whatever comes out of the environment.

In this sense, I-Organizations will be like basketball players, who have "instinctualized" a set of skills, to the point that they require no thinking at all and happen automatically: dribbling, passing, shooting, going up for a rebound, cutting through a defense.

The basketball players who are not able to develop these skills into instincts never become stars. They are constantly thinking about their actions. Meanwhile, the game is speeding past them. Their reactions—their reaction time—is always just a fraction of a second too slow. So they miss an opportunity.

I-Organizations will need to develop their instincts as well, and for exactly the same reasons. They will have to react instantly to either threat or opportunity, without any internal debates or rumination. In the even-faster world to come, if they don't react at light speed, they won't be first-string players. In the I-Age, even more than now, victory will belong to the swift.

Value Systems

Like transorganizations, and the organizations that came before them, I-Organizations will operate according to an internalized set of values. And in the I-Organization, most of these values will be familiar. But three, in particular, will be evolved versions of their current, somewhat undeveloped selves:

1. **Imperfection.** At first thought, it may be difficult to think of imperfection as a value, much less a useful one. And that mindset demonstrates how difficult a task it will be for the I-Organization to adopt this new view. But the simple truth is, the cost of attaining perfection and impeccability cannot be justified. Fixing those last few errors can add costs out of all proportion to the usefulness of something that is flawless.

   The truth is, and we all know it, most of the time, good enough is truly good enough. There's no need to wallpaper the inside of the closet, unless you're satisfying an obsession. It will hold just as many clothes, just as well and just as handily if it's merely painted a nice, neutral color. The same thing is true of practically every product or process ever invented.

   Imperfection is so commonplace, in fact, and so expected, that very few people ever notice it, as long as the product or service is good enough to accomplish its purpose. That means that money spent in the vain attempt at attaining perfect is wasted. It goes unnoticed. I-Organizations will understand this and incorporate it into their operational philosophy, resisting the urge to aspire to the unattainable and pursuing the goal of producing insignificant imperfections.

2. **Integral Individuality.** It is a daunting challenge for any organization to simultaneously embrace individuality and diversity and at the same time retain its own integrity and distinct identity. And this challenge is complicated by the urge to base organizational identity on a brand.

When an organization bases its identity on its brand, it means that all of its values, people and operations must align with brand identity. A better way is to identify the organization's intrinsic identity and to base brands and products on the identity that already exists.

I-Organizations will build identity and differentiation based on their souls, not their products, choosing or adjusting their products to meet their values, not the other way around. That is the surest way to avoid a conflict between who the organization is and what it does.

3. **Integrity-gravity.** Into the heady mix of intuition and instinct, interacting with others in real-time, acting more like a biological entity than a human construct, the I-Organization will take on one more task, a task that, if ignored, can bring down the whole edifice. That is, to act at all times with integrity, according to a set of moral values that build loyalty, pride and commitment. This is challenging for I-Organizations in much the same way it is challenging for individual human beings, and when the challenge is met, it is rewarding in much the same way, making the hard work that much more fulfilling.

Afterword

We have an imperfect, positive duty to seek our own perfection and the happiness of others.
Immanuel Kant

Some of the people who read this book—especially younger people—will find it an affirmation of their instincts and beliefs. Some will find much of what we've discussed new, but sensible. And, we suspect, another group—especially those who have decades of leadership under their belts—may find it radical, and in direct conflict with what they've learned over the years, or what think they've learned.

To all of these groups, we'd like to say that we've seen the ideas espoused here put to work in a wide variety of SMBs, government agencies and NGOs. They work. They can improve efficiency, productivity and profits. They can also improve job satisfaction and working relationships. They can make a positive impact on everyone, from the organization's leadership to its lowest level employees.

Strategy, Leadership and the Soul, at its core, asks you to think about your organization, your people and yourself in new and deeper ways.

It is a call to thoroughly perceiving both the outer world and the inner world, and to unite these understandings.

It is a call to consciousness.

It is a call to personal responsibility.

It is a call to harmonize your organization.

It is a call to elevate your people.

It is a call to know your soul and the soul of the organization, and to see that it is at the heart of everything you do.

It is a call to embrace diversity and encourage it.

It is a call to use your energy wisely.

It is also a call to make flexibility and adaptability a core competence.

It is a call to share power in order to multiply organizational strength.

Finally, it is a call to consider your possibilities unlimited.

Once upon a time, if you were the strongest beast, you could be pretty sure of winning. Later, you won by dominating through wealth. After that, in the age of international corporations and conglomerates, size meant victory. Today, whoever has the most information or customer knowledge will come out ahead.

But this paradigm is undergoing another change. Tomorrow, we are convinced, the organizations with the clearest understanding of reality and with the highest consciousness will be the winners because they will be able to see signs that are invisible to others.

This is your challenge.

Recommended Reading

Business Books

Presence—Human Purpose and the Field of the Future, Peter M. Senge, C. Otto Scharmer, Joseph Jaworski, Betty Sue Flowers. Society for Organizational Learning, Inc., 2004.

The Fifth Discipline, Peter M. Senge. Doubleday/Currency, 1994.

Organizing Genius, Charles Handy, Warren Bennis, Patricia Ward Biederman. Perseus, 1997.

Emotional Branding—How Successful Brands Gain the Irrational Edge. Daryl Travis, Prima Tech, 2000.

The Elephant and the Dragon—The Rise & Fall of India & China and What That Means for All of Us. Robyn Meredith, W. W. Norton & Company, Inc., 2007.

Scanning the Future—20 Eminent Thinkers on the World of Tomorrow, edited by Yorick Blumenfield. Thames & Hudson, 1999.

The Ultimate Question, Fred Reichheld. Harvard Business School Publishing Corporation, 2006.

Corporate Agility, Charles E. Grantham, James Ware, Cory Williamson. AMACOM, a division of American Management Association, 2007.

Communication Catalyst, Mickey Connolly and Richard Rianoshek. Kaplan Business, 2002.

Clicks and Mortar—Passion Driven Growth in an Internet Driven World, David S. Pottruck and Terry Pearce. The Jossey-Bass Business & Management Series, 2000.

The Synergy Trap, Mark L. Sirower. The Free Press, 1997.

Mobilizing Minds, Lowell L. Bryan and Claudia I. Joice. McGraw-Hill, 2007.

Platform for Change, Stafford Beer. John Wiley & Sons, 1975.

Seeing What's Next—using the theories of innovation to predict industry change, Clayton Christensen, Scott Anthony, Erik A. Roth. Harvard Business School Press, 2004.

A New Earth—awakening to your life's purpose, Eckhart Tolle. Plume Printing, 2006.

Competition—the birth of a new science, James Case. Hill and Wang, 2007.

Competition Demystified—a radically simplified approach to business strategy, Bruce Greenwald and Judd Kahn. Portfolio, 2005.

Leading Leaders, Jeswald W. Salacuse. AMACOM, 2006.

The Seven-Day Weekend, Ricardo Semler. Portfolio, 2004.

A Whole New Mind, Daniel Pink. Berkley Publishing Group, 2005.

Hidden in Plain Sight, Erich Joachimsthaler. Harvard Business School Press, 2007.

Crossing the Unknown Sea: Work as a Pilgrimage to Identity, David Whyte. Riverhead Books (a member of Penguin Putman Inc.), 2001.

The Heart Aroused, David Whyte. Currency Doubleday, 1994.

Change Your Thoughts—Change Your Life, Wayne Dyer. Hay House Publishers, 2007.

Management F-Laws: how organisations really work, Russ Ackoff, Herbert Addison and Sally Bibb. Triarchy Press 2007.

Philosophy and Science

The Five Dialogues, Plato, around 400 BC.

Discourse on Method and Meditations on First Philosophy, Rene Descartes, 1637.

Groundwork in Metaphysics of Morals, Immanuel Kant, 1785.

Critique of Practical Reason, Immanuel Kant, 1788.

On Liberty, John Mill Stuart. Cambridge University Press, 1989.

The Problems of Philosophy, Bertrand Russell, 1912.

Pragmatism, William James. Dover Publications, 1995.

I and Thou, Martin Buber. Continuum International Publishing Group Ltd., 1970.

Atlas Shrugged, Ayn Rand. Penguin Classics, 1957.

Human, All Too Human, Nietzsche. Various editions.

The Human Condition, Hannah Arendt. Chicago University Press, 2nd revised edition, 1999.

Existentialism & Human Emotions, Jean Paul Sartre, 1957.

Zen and the Art of Motorcycle Maintenance, Robert Pirsig. Corgi, 1976.

Goedel, Escher and Bach—an eternal golden braid, Douglas Hofstadter. Penguin, 1980.

Complexity—a Guided Tour, Melanie Mitchell. Oxford University Press, 2009.

Koby Huberman

Koby Huberman has more than 27 years' experience in global high-tech technology corporations, where he has held executive roles in general management, business development, strategy development, mergers and acquisitions and strategic marketing. He is known as a visionary business leader, and has helped many corporations through successful transformation to achieve accelerated growth.
Today he invests in emerging start-ups with disruptive breakthroughs, and continues to consult CEOs of global companies. His expertise spans several domains.

In parallel to his business career, Koby has been engaged in more than 25 voluntary projects with various NGOs and NFP organizations. As a strong believer in the leadership role of independent citizens in a modern civil society, his current activities focus on transformational initiatives for peace and prosperity in the Middle East.

He is the co-author of the proposed Israeli Peace Initiative (IPI), together with Yuval Rabin. He helped build Al-Bawader, the first venture capital group to invest in the Arab sector in Israel and, most recently, co-founded The Empathy Group Ltd.

His life-changing experience was a 450-mile walk in 1980, from the north edge of Israel to its south edge. This profound physical and mental challenge has shaped his business and leadership thinking, focusing on the combination of setting ambitious goals and developing the patience and commitment to achieve them.

Koby has a B.A. in Economics and Business, and an M.A. (magna cum laude) in Philosophy, both from Tel-Aviv University. He speaks several languages, and his hobbies include music, science, anthropology and mountain walks.

He is married to Tal, an artist, scholar and an architect. They have four children.

Jennifer Sertl

Jennifer Sertl is a thought leader in "corporate consciousness", where she bridges business strategy and neuroscience. She is the president and founder of Agility3R, an organizational effectiveness consulting firm, whose primary objective is aligning strategy and people to create customer value. Jennifer brings fifteen years of management-level experience supporting significant paradigm  shifts in both the telecommunications and health care industries. Her expertise lies in the coordination of executive leadership, shareholder responsibility, and employee engagement.

In addition, Jennifer has been very involved with Vistage International, the world's largest CEO membership organization, successfully moderating three CEO roundtables. She is a master facilitator for Renaissance Executive Forum. Jennifer travels extensively throughout the United States as a keynote speaker on "Agility-Resilience, Responsiveness, and Reflection for a Global Economy".

Jennifer holds a B.A. in English and a B.A. in existential philosophy, summa cum laude, from the University of Colorado at Boulder. Jennifer is actively involved in her community and serves on several boards. Her personal commitments include the Mental Health Association and Young Entrepreneurs Academy.

She lives in Rochester, NY with her husband Eric and three children.

In praise of *Strategy, Leadership and the Soul*:

I love this book! It bursts with fresh ideas and redefines what a true leader is today - and more importantly tomorrow. This book is pure gold for any business wanting enduring success.
Daniel C. Barnett, CEO, The Primavera Company
Speaker, Vistage International, Inc.

As you read this book, you realize that this is a new paradigm for business leadership – a sort of new breakthrough in "organizational mathematics". The book offers a sensitive and accurate viewpoint of all the factors which compose the newly regenerated version of the business world; a world where small and agile businesses, closer to their customers and able to provide flexible solutions to their customer needs, are going to leapfrog and bypass the established "experienced" business giants that are too slow to figure out what is happening out there. The three anchors in the book – Strategy, Leadership and the Soul – provide the coordinates to understand the new organizational dimensions. Beyond intellectually enjoying the original analyses in the book, I gained a new "GPS", which helps me "recalculate a new route" in any dynamically changing situation.
Ofer Levy, Chairman of the Lotem Group

The world needs leaders who understand and thrive on diversity and constant change. Most of us fall into the trap of looking for solutions for our companies; few of us look for ways of transforming ourselves first, so we can continually transform our businesses.

'People are our Business' should be the intrinsic belief of every executive that strives for the sustainability of their business. As the authors very eloquently put it, moving away from "command and control" to "communicate and enroll" is essential today, as is engaging all employees in strategy conversations. This is a book for everybody that believes that business sustainability, in the uncertain times we live in, is possible.
Carl R. Luttig, Managing Director of the ZEAL Group Pty Ltd., Melbourne, Australia

Strategy, Leadership and the Soul presents an insightful view of the future that will be embraced by transleaders and create bewilderment for those who cannot make the transition to a world where customer knowledge and desires set the pace for value creation".
Rick Plympton, CEO, Optimax Systems Inc.

Humbleness and leadership – two words seemingly from different sides of personality. Can they be at peace with one another, or better still, can they create a harmonious combination?

As CEOs in today's world, we need to allow the collective and individual creative intelligence of our employees to shine like never before. We need to enable greatness in others by giving them the opportunity to express themselves while we provide the foresight for a greater future. This book shows you how to do this. Let it also drive you to self reflect on who YOU are and who YOU want to be as you prepare for your next challenge.
Gabi Seligsohn, CEO of Nova Measurement Instruments Ltd.

In today's world, the 'business book of the week' usually espouses a new quick solution to problems or better ways to restructure your business in 90 minutes or less. This is a refreshing new book that asks questions, important questions that we really need to know the answers to - answers that we know, but don't know how to get to easily. It helps us to understand our business, and how our own personal wattage affects outcomes. It makes us think differently. It makes us answer tough questions. Read it twice!
Peter Parts, Peter Parts Electronics

Strategy, Leadership, and the Soul is a timely and prescient addition to the business knowledge landscape. It is often difficult to understand the complexities and subtleties of the changing business environment while struggling to cope with our own internal operations and preconceived mental models. This book clarifies the factors causing dramatic transformation in the economy and society, and provides a guide for both the personal and the organizational adaptation needed to meet the challenges of the future.
 Dale Ewing, CEO/President, InstallNet